The Monastery of
Saint
Catherine

The Monastery of
Saint Catherine

EDITED BY

ORIANA BADDELEY AND EARLEEN BRUNNER

THE SAINT CATHERINE FOUNDATION

The Monastery of Saint Catherine was published to
accompany an exhibition at the
Foundation for Hellenic Culture, London,
June–July 1996
HB ISBN 0 9528063 0 4
SB ISBN 0 9528063 1 2
© The Saint Catherine Foundation 1996

Designed by Michael Hutchins
Typesetting and page production by The Chimæra Press
Printed by Watmoughs Corporate Print
Bound by Watmoughs Corporate Print,
Woolnough Bookbinding and the Fine Bindery

The exhibition and this book were sponsored by

EUROPEAN FINANCIAL
GROUP EFG

Contents

Illustrations

All photographs except those on pages 30, 48–50, 57, 78–111 were taken by Garry McNamara

Acknowledgements

THE SAINT CATHERINE FOUNDATION has been formed in order to assist the monks of the monastery in their task as custodians of its unique and priceless heritage, and our first thanks are to them and to his eminence Archbishop Damianos.

One of the first acts of the Foundation has been to support the initiative of HRH the Prince of Wales in arranging for the training of one of the monks in conservation techniques. The internship of Father Nilus at the School of Art History and Conservation at Camberwell College of Arts, a college of the London Institute, was complemented by a research visit by experts from Camberwell to help with an assessment and analysis of conservation issues at the monastery. The Foundation would like to thank Professor Roger Breakwell for supporting the work of the research team, and the team themselves, Richard Hughes, David Collins and Michael Hutchins, for their expertise and advice. During their visit and throughout the arrangements for Father Nilus' internship the British Council at Alexandria has been very supportive, and particular thanks go to their representative Valerie Teague.

The British Ambassador in Cairo, Mr Christopher Long, and his staff, particularly Steven Graham, must also be thanked.

The final member of the Camberwell team was the photographer Garry McNamara, whose work not only illustrates this book but has also formed an important part of the conservation report.

The publication of this book commemorates the launch of the Saint Catherine Foundation and accompanies an exhibition about the Monastery held at the Foundation for Hellenic Culture, London. Throughout the organisation of the exhibition we have had great support from the monastery and its representatives, and particular thanks go to Nicolas Vadis for all his help.

The staff of the Foundation for Hellenic Culture and their director Dr Jenni Richardson have embraced the project with great enthusiasm and committed many hours of work to its success. Eve Graves and Keith Cavers have advised and helped in the planning of the exhibition in ways too numerous to list.

Many thanks also go to Mr Dimitri Dondos and all the staff of Bridgewater House for their generous participation in the launching of the Saint Catherine Foundation.

The book itself is the product of the tireless efforts of Michael Hutchins and Earleen Brunner who have worked with great skill and speed to do justice to the erudite and illuminating texts of the contributing authors.

Nothing, however, would have been possible without the committed and sustained support of Dr and Mrs S. J. Latsis and our sponsors The European Financial Group EFG to whom we offer our grateful thanks.

In 1995, during a tour of Egypt, I had the great good fortune to visit the Monastery of St Catherine in the Sinai desert. The monks extended to me the heart warming hospitality which, for centuries, they have shown to all pilgrims. The monastery is the site of one of the oldest Christian communities in the world and the monks of St Catherine's are the guardians of a tradition of Christian piety that has lasted continuously for almost 2,000 years, as well as being the custodians of a unique collection of icons and early manuscripts from the Christian, Islamic and Judaic traditions.

I was deeply moved by the sense of continuity and timelessness which imbues the monastery and its surroundings, from which so many have drawn inspiration. However, it was also apparent that the incursions of the modern world have imposed considerable strains on St Catherine's. In the last twenty years tourism has had an impact on the spiritual and physical life of the monastery that 2,000 years of the currents of human history have been unable to destroy. The traditional life of the monastery is now at risk, not only because the monastic vocation is disrupted by the large number of tourists, but also because the very weight of visitors is itself introducing new conservation problems into the rarefied atmosphere of Mount Sinai. The threat to the priceless heritage of icons and relics and to the manuscripts which not only underpin the Christian faith, but are of great significance to Judaism and Islam, is a very real one. The faith and resilience of the monks of St Catherine's have ensured the survival of this legacy, but they need our support in this great task.

The St Catherine Foundation has been set up with the aim of assisting the monks to continue the work that they have undertaken for centuries, and to ensure the survival of this unique monument to human faith.

An Introduction to the Monastery of Saint Catherine

HIS EMINENCE, ARCHBISHOP DAMIANOS

ENCIRCLED BY THE GRANITE MOUNTAINS and inhospitable desert expanses of the Sinai Peninsula, the Holy Monastery of Saint Catherine stands beneath Mount Sinai, where God walked. Saint Catherine's is the oldest and most important continuously inhabited Christian monastery in the world. The spiritual, monastic and philanthropic life that began here at the end of the third century AD endures to the present day. By the year 400, so the narrative of the Spanish noblewoman Etheria informs us, there was a small church in existence on the peak of Mount Sinai, another one lower down at Horiv and third, with a very beautiful garden, near Vato. The church near Vato must be the one which, according to tradition, Saint Helena founded. That church had a tower, as did the one near Vato, a fact confirmed by the archaeological record.

Monastic life proper began with the construction of the fortified monastery and magnificent basilica under Justinian the Great in the middle of the sixth century. While a number of holy men lived on in solitude in the dispersed hermitages surrounding the monastery, the main coenobite community came together under a uniform rule. Some remarkable men served as abbot: Doulas, Longinos, Anastasius (later Patriarch of Antioch), Saint John Klimakos, author of the *Spiritual Ladder*, and the other Anastasius, author of the *Guide*.

Spiritual life flourished through the upheaval of the Arab conquest (AD 641). The monks of Sinai maintained good relations both with the Muslim rulers of the peninsula and with the desert tribesmen, to whom the monks expressed their sincere charity, distributing food to the hungry. During this difficult period, the monastery attracted the religious and reverent interest of all Christendom.

With the discovery of the relics of Saint Catherine, the Alexandrian martyr, the fame of Mount Sinai and the monastery grew. At the beginning of the eleventh century, a certain Simeon Pentaglossos, a holy monk from Sicily whose name suggests that he could speak five languages, travelled to the West, taking with him relics of the martyred Catherine and spreading the worship of the saint wherever he went. The monastery enjoyed friendly relations with the whole of western Christianity, relations that endured long after schism divided the Orthodox and Latin churches.

The Holy Monastery of Sinai has maintained its independence since the sixth century. The administrative head of the monastic order of Saint Catherine, the abbot, initially held the rank of bishop. Sometime between the eleventh and twelfth century, the abbot was granted the title of archbishop, to facilitate the ordination of priests. The Archbishop of Sinai is ordained by the Patriarch of Jerusalem, and the archbishop commemorates the patriarch during church services. Due to the autonomous status of the monastery, the archbishop does not participate in the Synod of Jerusalem.

Monasticism prospered in the harsh desert environment of the Sinai. The rich grace derived from the many Epiphanies in the Old Testament allowed a growing number of ascetics to follow Christ, achieving a deep spirituality. They took as their central purpose purification through prayer and fasting, aspiring in all humility to the secret union of the soul with the divine Trinity through Christ.

From its earliest beginnings, the Sinai monastery produced some important spiritual and contemplative teachers of prayer: Nilus, Saint John Klimakos, Hesychios of Vato and the two Anastasiuses. After them came Filotheos of Sinai, Gregory and others. Their writings, especially those of Saint John Klimakos, met the spiritual needs of all Christians in search God's truth. Among these holy fathers were some whose message reached well beyond Sinai, notably the Anastasius who taught in the seventh century and Gregory the Sinaite, an influential expositor of the thirteenth century. In all, some two hundred holy men, many of them anonymous, lived an exemplary life in the Sinai, bearing Christian witness. The Orthodox Church honours the saints of the Sinai every year, on the first Wednesday following Easter.

Throughout the monastery's long history, the monks of Saint Catherine's have maintained strong bonds with the bedouin tribespeople of South Sinai. Of the six main tribes that inhabit an area covering some thirty thousand square kilometres, the oldest and most closely associated with the monastery is the Jabaliya. This tribe claims descent from some two hundred military families despatched to Mount Sinai by the Emperor Justinian to protect the monks from barbarian incursions. Attacked twice in the fourth century by the Saracens and Blemmyans, the monks took the possibility of invasion seriously. In the decades that followed the Arab conquest, the bedouin converted to Islam. Their Muslim faith brought a new spiritual dimension to the Sinai, symbolized by the mosque that has stood within the monastery walls since the eleventh century, in an outstanding example of mutual tolerance and respect.

The bedouin and the monastery have long enjoyed a symbiotic relationship. The monastery, ever a stabilizing force in the Sinai, habitually mediated disputes between the bedouin, defining tribal boundaries for example. Through the centuries the holy fathers have extended their charitable assistance to the bedouin, providing them with medical care in particular. Near neighbours, the monks and the Jabaliya have rejoiced and mourned together, sharing their happiness and sorrow. The monastery was represented at Jabaliya weddings, funerals and other ceremonies, some of which incorporated vestiges of ancient Christian customs.

From the eighth century to the middle of the twentieth (when the automobile first made its appearance at Mount Sinai), the bedouin transported supplies to the monastery by camel train. From Cairo or the Suez Canal, it was a difficult ten-day journey across the desert to Saint Catherine's. Over the years, a system developed whereby all the tribes of the Sinai shared equally, both in the work and in the profits of the transport trade.

As monastic life developed in the mountainous Sinai region, workshops were established at Saint Catherine's for the copying of service books and patristic texts, and for the production of icons and liturgical objects destined for the use of an expanding religious community. The treasures that survive from the Byzantine past have been gathered up for safekeeping within the monastery compound. The library houses a rare collection of codices and scrolls dating back to the fourth century AD, including many fine manuscripts copied at Saint Catherine's from the tenth century onwards. A large archive of documents derives from the monastery's dependencies in the Sinai and around the world and from other sources, ecclesiastical and secular.

The unique icon collection comprises the few sixth- and seventh-century encaustic icons to have survived the scourge of iconoclasm, as well as a comprehensive selection of icons in the tempera technique illustrating the development of the Byzantine style from the eighth century to the present day. The monks perfected their art in workshops situated not only at Saint Catherine's, but also in the monastery's many dependencies. The monastery at Iraklion in Crete where the painter El Greco studied was connected to Saint Catherine's.

Many superb examples of Orthodox art have been preserved in the dry climate and clean air of the Sinai. Perhaps the greatest testament to the Byzantine past is the fabric of the monastery itself, above all Justinian's basilica and fortified sixth-century buildings. Taken as a whole, Saint Catherine's represents a unique monument to Orthodox monastic life.

Today, in the Monastery of Sinai, Orthodox monks, most of whom are Greek, perpetuate the tradition of Byzantine panel painting, although on a smaller scale than in the past. With the help and support of friends and donors, the monastery is engaged in the restoration of buildings and the conservation of manuscripts, icons and other artefacts by specialists using advanced technology. The holy fathers of Saint Catherine's are dedicated to the preservation of their spiritual heritage and the eternal values it embodies. They have separated themselves from the world, not to repudiate their responsibility towards others, but to affirm another way of life.

16

The Monastery of Saint Catherine: a Duality of Natures

RICHARD HUGHES

T HE MONASTERY OF SAINT CATHERINE lies at the head of the Wadi ad-Dayr, cradled between the jagged multiple granite peaks of the Jebel ad-Dayr and Jebel Musa (Moses' Mountain), where it has survived through fourteen centuries. A first encounter with the monastery conveys some of the paradox of this unique community. The site is an oasis, a Mediterranean island in the rugged wilderness of southern Sinai. As one ascends gently from lower down the valley the approach is screened by the monastery garden, which extends a tongue of cultivation down the rocky valley, and around the complex of low buildings outside the main walls. The character of the garden is set by the dominant, dark green cypress trees brought to the monastery from Mount Athos and Cyprus, and the sinuous, capped low walls that contain it and define its physical boundaries. Beyond the garden, set against a backdrop of boulder-strewn pink granite slopes, stand the high walls of the fortified monastery enclosure. It is at once unique to its location, fitted to the landscape of the valley, yet evoking a sense of otherness and recollections of connections with Greece, the Mediterranean and Palestine.

This curious sense of independence and strength of identity for the community is ultimately dependent on the political and economic vagaries of the outside world, with which it has been in constant communion and on which it has exerted a powerful influence and constitutes one of the central paradoxes of the monastery. Intended as a remote refuge of simplicity, tranquillity, silence, devotion and prayer in which monks could seek a closer communion with God, Saint Catherine's is nonetheless a force in the world.

THE MONASTERY OF
SAINT CATHERINE
The sharply defined outlines of the walled monastery and its outlying gardens and buildings nestling in the sloping basin of the Wadi ad-Dayr are clear from a high point on the Jebel ad-Dayr. The edge of the plain of el Raha can be seen in the far distance at the foot of the granite slopes.

Following page:
JUSTINIAN'S FORTIFIED
WALLS
The imposing walls, built by order of the Emperor Justinian in the sixth century, encompassed the biblical sites of the Burning Bush and the Well of Moses together with the fourth century church erected under the patronage of Helena, the mother of Constantine the Great. It created a fortress which both protected the monastic community and established a strategic outpost.

17

The power of the site itself and its rich associations with the biblical stories of Moses and Elijah created an early focus for religious activity and the establishment of a church alongside the Burning Bush and, subsequently, the familiar fortified monastery which survives to this day. At the outset the building ordered by the Emperor Justinian was made to serve both sacred and secular purposes. Constructed for the protection of the religious community, the monastery also functioned as a strategically positioned fortress. Its early dedication to the Mother of God, through symbolic association of the virgin birth with the bush that burned but was

THE CHAPEL OF SAINT STEPHEN
The interior of the monastery is reminiscent of a Greek village, with its mixture of buildings of all sizes, and narrow passageways. Vines grow in arbours and overhang the courtyard in front of the barrel-vaulted chapel of Saint Stephen in the southern part of the monastery.

not consumed by fire, was later overlaid with the tradition of the saintly Catherine, whose relics were transferred to the monastery from the summit of the nearby Jebel Katharina (Mount Catherine). The influence and power of Saint Catherine's legacy, which attracted a stream of pilgrims and worshippers to the monastery, symbolizes the relationship that the monastery still has with the outside world. Historically Saint Catherine's has survived the political changes that have affected the Sinai peninsula, even though these have called the future of the monastery into question time and again.

The monastery has nonetheless achieved a remarkable degree of autonomy. Although essentially subject to the doctrine and culture of Byzantine Orthodox Christianity, it stood apart from the eleventh-century schism which separated the Orthodox and Roman churches, and remained in communion with Rome. Through the centuries communication with Constantinople was severed and

THE CHARNEL HOUSE
The Charnel House, set against the dark cypresses which give the monastery the feel of the Mediterranean, is the repository of monks who died here over the centuries. It adjoins the cemetery in the monastery garden, where the dead are first buried before their bones are disinterred.

LIGHTING A CANDLE
One of the fathers places a votive candle in the candelium in front of the icon of Saint Catherine, in the narthex of the Church.

MAKING BREAD
*Each week the monks and the
Jabaliya Bedouin helpers
gather together in the bakery
to bake bread for the whole
community, unobtrusively
linking ancient traditions and
modern technology.
They knead and shape the
dough, working at floured
wooden boards, and transfer
the shaped masses to shallow
wooden moulds, hollowed
from beams, to prove.
The loaves are transferred
using long-handled flat
spatulas into the open kiln-
style baking oven, from which
they emerge as the familiar
coarse bread of the region.*

re-established several times, and links were forged with the churches in Palestine and Syria, and the Slavonic churches of the East.

Yet the sense of this persistence through change is not one of survival through isolation. An ability to embrace change, and an adaptation to the world as given, seen through the eyes of faith, has enabled the monks of Saint Catherine's to maintain a deeper tradition, to uphold a view of the world in which each of its particulars has meaning in the context of a sustained and focussed attempt to understand and encompass the nature of the relationship between God and man. The works of man as elements in that world appear as metaphors and parables of religious meaning that are embodied in the physical structure and use of icons, the writing and making of manuscripts and books, the interpretation of objects and events and the observances of daily life and sacred ritual.

Each week, for example, the monks and bedouin gather

MONASTERY BUILDINGS

The monastery has a wide range of styles of building, with some structures built of stone and wood framing, with wattle and daub or plaster infill. Such constructions may seem fragile but are in fact flexible enough to resist the earthquakes which affect the region, and can more easily be repaired.

There are also breeze block and concrete constructions, as in the covered areas protecting the massive winding gear which, until relatively recently, was used to haul goods and people up through a hatchway in the monastery's north wall.

together in the monastery bakery to make the bread for the whole community, in the timeless and natural co-operative rhythm of a familiar and cherished communal activity. Towards the end of the baking, some of the dough is kneaded separately and imprinted with religious images from a set of wooden stamps, some ancient, some new, for use in the holy communion. The infusion of this everyday secular activity with a moving but unemphasized sense of the sacred is matched by the extension of the material of everyday life into the liturgy.

The buildings of the monastery, constructed and modified in response to changing needs and fortunes, date from all periods. The walled fortress and the church built in the sixth century on the orders of the Emperor Justinian and his wife Theodora, incorporate the small fourth-century chapel on the original site of the Burning Bush, erected by Saint Helena. The mosque that stands within the walls was converted hurriedly in the eleventh century from

VISITORS TO THE
MONASTERY
*Each morning, except on
Sundays and holy festivals,
crowds of visitors enter the
monastery through the small
door in the north wall, close to
Kleber's Tower, and
congregate in the narrow
passageway next to the wall
of the church, moving on to
visit the Burning Bush, the
Well of Moses and the
interior of the basilica.*

Facing page:
CAMPANILE AND
MINARET
*The multi-denominational
character of the site is
emphasised by the
juxtaposition of the belltower, built in 1871 by
Gregorius, a Sinai monk, to
house bells presented by the
tsars of Russia, and the
minaret associated with a
mosque which was converted
from an existing building in
the eleventh century.*

an existing building, apparently to forestall a possible Muslim incursion. The old refectory with its gothic arches and engraved coats of arms dates from the time of the crusades. The north walls and tower were reconstructed at the behest of Napoleon, after they had crumbled at the end of the eighteenth century. The campanile was built by Gregorius in the nineteenth century to house bells given to the monastery by the Russian tsars, while the substantial south wing and loggia, site of the monks' quarters and the libraries, took shape in the mid-twentieth century.

All these developments represent the evolving life of the

SAINT CATHERINE'S
VILLAGE

*Some modern settlements are
now situated within two or
three kilometres of the
monastery, including the
village of Saint Catherine
and a recently-built tourist
village, which is located on the
plain of el Raha, the
traditional site of the Israelite
encampment in the time of
Moses.*

monastery, which has nonetheless retained its character and identity through change. The building outside the walls of a new dispensary to serve the local community continues the cycle of growth and renewal.

This does not imply a passive acceptance of the world, but an active engagement with an ideal of service and responsibility, that takes into account social and political realities. Saint Catherine's upholds the monastic tradition of hospitality, an expression of devotion through the material as well as the spiritual.

This engagement with an ideal of service continues to have a strong impact on the life of the monastery in the twentieth century, as the growth of access to the area increases and the monastery is included in an increasing number of tourist itineraries. As preservers of the multi-denominational religious sites that are encompassed within the monastery walls and throughout the surrounding area, the monks of Saint Catherine's welcome thousands of

28

High on the slopes of Jebel ad-Dayr trees grow sheltered by a huge cleft in the rock. The region is generally bare of trees but has a rich ecology of wild plants and herbs, some of which are gathered by the monks and used in the kitchen and dispensary.

visitors to the Well of Moses, the Burning Bush and the church of Saint Catherine itself. Sometimes this influx must seem akin to the historical pilgrimage and caravanserai tradition that marked an earlier phase of the monastery's history. Visitors lodge in the hostel and eat together in the refectory which, together with a few small shops, creates a cluster of low buildings outside the walls. They share the bread baked in the monastery ovens, before climbing the Path of Repentance, or ascending the camel path, to the peak of Mount Sinai. The conversation in the refectory reflects the wide range of reasons why people make their way to

29

Jabaliya Bedouin rest in the shade of the garden arbour at the outlying monastery settlement at the Faran Oasis, one of a network of gardens cultivated in the region. Faran was at one time a flourishing settlement and the site of the Archbishop's residence.

Saint Catherine's. Many are modern pilgrims who may have come from Greece, or who have travelled via Palestine and the Holy Land on a long route, and whose visit brings to life the familiar stories of their various faiths. For others the journey is secular rather than sacred, but each in their own way is seeking some meaning in an encounter with ancient tradition, in the modern world.

That world is encroaching. Visible from the top of the monastery walls is a tourist village, situated on the plain of el Raha, where the Israelites are said to have camped while Moses ascended the mountain.

Coaches with their modern caravans of tourists approach from the valley, passing Aaron's chapel in the middle distance. In addition to the pressures from tourism, an increasing number of scholars are demanding access to the monastery's unique collection of manuscripts and icons. The brotherhood of monks is conscious of its acknowledged responsibility to the religious heritage and treasures

it protects, and acutely aware of what this might mean for Saint Catherine's ability to sustain its monastic tradition in the future. How will it be possible to accommodate the demands of tourism and scholarship with the ideals of monastic life?

The balance of forces is crucial. The monastery has survived like a well-adapted organism in a human ecology, maintaining a harmonious relationship with its broader socio-cultural and spiritual environment. At times during Saint Catherine's history, these relationships have been as precarious as the natural ecology of the Sinai, where for example, the use of wood as fuel stripped the region of trees. The population of monks has fluctuated radically, so that at times the monastery has barely survived. The continuation of Saint Catherine's has depended on the creation of a network of relations which extend beyond the monastery walls and, indeed, far beyond Sinai. For material and spiritual support has been provided through the widespread

THE HERMITAGE OF
FATHER ADRIANOS
The hermitage is one of many associated with the monastery. Father Adrianos lived alone here for many years and tended the small garden in this steeply sloping valley among the granite peaks above the monastery.

31

Metochia (daughter houses) established in Egypt, Persia, Crete and Jerusalem, for example, a small number of which survive to this day. A comparison can be drawn with the local cultivation of oases as gardens, islands of horticulture which must be carefully maintained against the surrounding environment.

Globally, in a world which has experienced a communications revolution, the supporting network is created through the widespread dissemination of information about the monastery, its traditions and holdings.

This brings with it the danger of ever-increasing demands on a small community: reciprocal concern for the preservation of Saint Catherine's unique heritage is accompanied

... τοῦ ἐπισκόπου ἡμῶν τοῦ δεῖνος·
ὑπὲρ τοῦ ἁγίου οἴκου τούτου καὶ τῶν με-
ὑπὲρ τοῦ ἀρχιεπισκόπου ἡμῶν τοῦ δεῖνος πάσης
τῆς ἐπισκοπῆς τοῦ πρεσβυτερίου τῆς ἐν χ(ριστ)ῷ
ὑπὲρ τῶν εὐσεβεστάτων καὶ θεοφιλ-
ὑπὲρ τοῦ σωθῆναι λαὸν ἡμῶν τοῦ δεῖνος
ὑπὲρ τῆς ἁγίας μονῆς ἡμῶν τοῦ τόπου πα-
ὑπὲρ εὐκρασίας ἀέρων εἰρφοριας τ
ὑπὲρ πλεόντων ὁδοιπορούντων νοσ-
ὑπὲρ τοῦ ῥυσθῆναι ἡμᾶς ἀπὸ πάσης

ἀντιλαβοῦ σῶσον· Τῆς παναγίας·
Ἐκφώνησις· Ὅτι πρέπει σοι πᾶσα δ-
ὁ δ(ιάκονο)ς αμ(ήν)· ἱε(ρεὺς)· Εἰρήνη πᾶσι καὶ τῷ πν(εύματ)ι·
εἰ δέ ἐστιν ἀρχ(ιερεὺς) λέγει τὸ μάλιστα
καὶ τὰ ἑξῆς ἕως τοῦ καθίσματος· λέ-
τοῖς ἱε(ρεῦσι)· ἐπὶ καὶ ἐπ' ἐμψήχων αἰτῶν
Τῆς παναγίας δ(έσποινα)· Ἐκφώνησις·
Ὅτι σὸν τὸ ἱερατός καὶ σοῦ ἐστιν ἡ βα-
εἰ δέ ἐστιν τὸ χ(αῖρε) ἐχε... βα·
ψάλλονται τὰ ψ(αλμ)... τὸ ἐν τοῦ τρισ-
καὶ τὰ πρὸς ὁ λε... λο μεγαλον·

εἰ δέ ἐστιν δόξα εἰς αἰνῆτ... θ(εό)ν ...
ἐπὶ τὰς εἰ μεγάλας ... ὅδος ... ἀπ' οὐ ἱε(ρεὺς)
εὐχὴ τοῦ θυμιάματος καὶ κρίοτ· λε-
γομένου τοῦ ἱε(ρέ)ω... τ ... ἡν δέχην·
... θεὸς καὶ σωτῆρι καὶ μέσον ἡμ(ῶν)
ας· αἱ π... εὐχόμεθα ὑπὲρ· ...
ρίζομεν καὶ δεόμεθα σοῦ ... ά-
τα τῶν αἰτῶν τῶν· κατὰ θῦμον
τὴν προσφ... ἡμῖν εἰς ὀσμὴν εὐωδία
καὶ ἐν δ... όμισόν σου· καὶ ἐκ τῆς ἐκκ(λησίας)

...
...
ὁ θ(εὸ)ς ... μενος ...
αίωνος τοῦ αἰ...

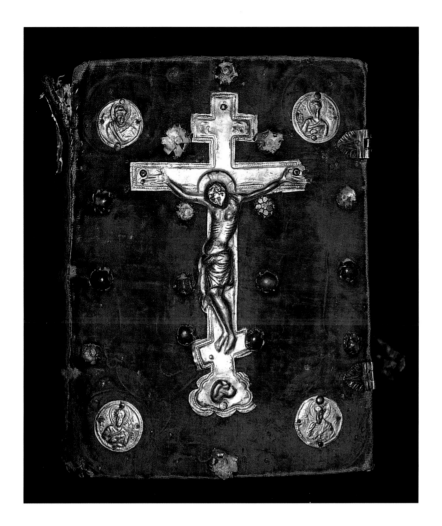

by the need for balance, the need to achieve a sustainable relationship with the world.

The world-famous library of Saint Catherine's serves as an example, both of the way in which an active engagement with the world has sustained a heritage, and of the challenge the monastery faces. The library is unique in terms of its longevity and continuous history, as well as in the composition of its holdings, which reflect the importance of the monastery as a place of pilgrimage and its interaction with the distinct traditions of Orthodoxy. Although the early history of the library is not known, it is likely that it was furnished with a significant collection of books at the time of the monastery's consolidation as an imperial foundation under the patronage of Justinian and Theodora. The subsequent political fluctuations in Sinai and in the parallel

history of Orthodoxy created the pattern of changing influence, patronage and contact that has shaped the collection. Thus, in addition to the uniquely rich collection of early Greek manuscripts, the extensive Arabic holdings, for example, are crucial to the study of early Christian Arabic literature. Following the Arab dominion of the area, which for a time effectively severed links with Constantinople, imperial protection and the Byzantine world, there was a marked shift in orientation towards the Christian centres in Palestine, and the Greek Patriarchate of Jerusalem in particular, with which the monastery still maintains its closest links, a connection represented in the library holdings. In addition there are substantial and important collections of Syriac, Georgian, Aramaic, Russian and Slavonic manuscripts, which provide similar material signs of the richness and diversity of the monastery's historical interactions.

The collection also reflects the different functions served by its holdings of codices (bound manuscripts) and printed books. These include their liturgical use in support of church services and monastic observance; a more general

ΝΑΙΚΩ...ΙϹΗΟΛ
ΟΥϹΚΑΙΕΝΕΚΛΕΙ
ϹΩΘΕΝΑΥΤΩΝ ΤΗ
ΚΑΙΑΝΕΚΗϹΑΝ
ΠΙΤΟΛΩΜΑΤΟΥΠ
ΓΟΥΤΟΥΕΜΠΡΗϹΑΙ
ΑΥΤΟΝΕΝΠΥΡΙ
ΚΑΙΕΡΡΙΨΕΝΓΥΝΗ
ΜΙΑΚΛΑϹΜΑΕΠΙ
ΜΥΛΙΟΥΕΠΙΚΕΦΑ
ΛΗΝΑΚΙΜΕΛΕΧ
ΚΑΙΕΚΛΑϹΕΝΤΟ
ΚΡΑΝΙΟΝΑΥΤΟΥ
ΚΑΙΕΒΟΗϹΕΝΤΑ
ΧΥΠΡΟϹΤΟΠΑΙΔΑ
ΡΙΟΝΤΟΑΙΡΟΝΤΑ
ϹΚΕΥΗΑΥΤΟΥΚΑΙ
ΕΙΠΕΝΑΥΤΩϹΠΑ
ϹΟΝΤΗΝΡΟΜΦΑΙ
ΑΝϹΟΥΚΑΙΘΑΝΑ
ΤΩϹΟΝΜΕΜΗΠ
ΤΕΕΙΠΩϹΙΝΓΥΝΗ
ΑΠΕΚΤΕΙΝΕΝΑΥ
ΚΑΙΕΞΕΚΕΝΤΗ
ΑΥΤΟΝΤΟΠΑΙΔΑ
ΟΝΑΥΤΟΥΚΑΙΑΠΕ
ΘΑΝΕΝ·
ΚΑΙΙΔΕΝΑΝΗΡΙϹΛ
Ο...ΑΠΕΘΑΝ ΕΝ
ΑΒΙΜΕΛΕΧ...
...
ΠΑΤΡΙΑΥΤΟΥΤΟΑ
ΚΤΕΙΝΑΙΤΟΥϹΟ
ΡΛΟΜΗΚΟΝΤΑ
ΑΔΕΛΦΟΥϹΑΥΤ
ΚΑΙΤΗΝΠΑϹΑΝ
ΠΟΝΗΡΙΑΝΑΝ
ΑΡΩΝϹΥΧΕΜΕ
ϹΤΡΕΨΕΝΟΘ
ΚΕΦΑΛΗΝΑΥΤ
ΚΑΙΕΠΗΛΘΕ
ΠΑΥΤΟΥ ΚΑΙ

ΠΕΡΙΚΑΛ...
ΚΝΑΠΑΝΕϹΤΙΜΕ
ΑΚΙΜΕΛΕΧΤΟΥ
ϹΑΠΤΟΝΙϹΛΩΘΑ
ΥΙΟϹΡΟΥΑΓΙΟϹ ΝΑ
ΤΡΑΛΕϹΑΦΟΤΑ
ΑΝΗΡΙϹΑΧΑΡΚΑ
ΑΥΤΟϹΩΚΕΙΕΝΑ
ΜΕΙΡΕΝΟΡΕΦΟ
ΚΑΙΕΚΡΙΝΑΝΤΟΝ
ΙϹΧΕΙΚΟϹΙΤΡΙ
ΤΗΚΑΙΑΠΕΘΑΝ Ν
ΚΑΙΕΤΑΦΗΕΝϹΑ
ΜΕΙΡ...
ΚΑΙΑΝ ΕϹΤΗ
ΤΑΠΤΩΝΙϹΧΕΙΡΟ
ΑΛΛΑΚΑΙ Ο ΥΙ Ν
ΤΟΝΙϹΧΕΙΚΟϹΙ
ΟΕΤΗΚΑΙΕΘΑΝΑ
ΤΩΤΡΙΑΚΟΝΤΑΑ
ΟΥΙΟΙϹΕΠΙΚΑΙΝΟΝ
ΤΕϹΕΠΙΤΡΙΑΚΟΝΤΑ
ΑΥΟΠΩΛΟΥϹΚΑΙ
ΤΡΙΑΚΟΝΤΑΠΟΛ
ΑΥΤΟΙϹΑΥΛΕΙϹ
ΚΕΤΕΚΤΗϹΑΜ
ΑϹΤΑΘΙϹΑΝΕΝ
ΓΑΛΑΑΝΟΙϹΑΝΘ
ΒΑΝΕΝΤΕϹΚΑΙ
ΚϹΤΕΘΕΝΡΑΜΝ
ΕΠΕϹΟϹΘΕΝΤ
ΕΚΕΝΙΟΝΙΟΝ Ν
ΕΚΛΑϹΩΚΑΙΤΟ
ΑΘΟϹΙΟΡΕΤΟΥ
ΟΕΠΙΕϹϹΑϹΚΝΟϹ
ΙϹΤΟϹϹΟΘΕΟϹΕΜ
ΑΚΚΑΙΤΟΙϹΘΕΟΙϹ
ΘΠΛΑΜΜΩΝΚΑΙ
ΤΟΙϹΘΕΟΙϹΙϹ
ϹΤΙΒΙΜΚΑΙΕΝΚΑ
ΤΕΛΙΠΟΝΤΟΝΚ
ΚΑΙΟΥΚΕΛΟΥ

ϹΑΝΑ...
ΚΑΙΟΤΙΤΟΥϹ...
ΚΟΙΝΑΠΟΥ...
ΚΙΟΥ... Ν
ΟΠΕΡΙ ΓΦ...
ΜΟΝΑΙϹΕΟΝΝ
ΚΑΙΕΜΑΛΑϹΕΝΤ
ΥΙΟΥϹΙϹΕΛΟΤ
ΟΥϹΚΩΠΟΛΕΝΧ
ΚΤΩΕΠΤΑΕΤΗ
ΤΑϹΥΙΟΥϹΙϹΤΟΥ
ΕΝΤΩΠΕΡΑΝΤΟΥ
ΙΟΡΔΑΝΟΥΕΝΤΗΓΗ
ΤΟΥΑΜΟΡΡΙΤΟΥΕΝ
ΓΑΛΑΑΚΑΙΔΙΕΒΗ
ϹΑΝΟΙ ΥΙΟΙ ΑΜΜ
ΤΟΝΙΟΡΔΑΝΗΝΗΙΑ
ΡΑΤΑϹΑϹΘΑΙΠΡΟϹ
ΙΟΥΔΑΝ
ΚΑΙΕΝΙΑΜΕΙΝ
ΚΑΙΠΡΟϹΕΦΡΑΙΜ
ΚΑΙΕΘΛΙΒΗΙϹ
ϹΦΟΔΡΑΚΑΙΕΒΟΗϹΑΝ
ΤΟΝΙϹΧΙΡΟϹ
ϹΥΛΕΓΟΝΤΕϹΗΜ
ΤΟΜΕΝϹΟΙΟΤΙΕΝ
ΚΑΤΕΛΙΠΟΜΕΝΤ
ΘΝ ΚΝ ΙΕΔΟΥΛΕΥϹΑ
ΜΕΝΤΩΚΑΛΕΙΜ
ΚΑΙΕΙΠΕΝΚϹΠΡΟ
ΤΟΥϹΥΙΟΥϹΙϹ ΜΗ
ΟΥΧΙΕϹΕΙΥΠΤΟΥ
ΑΠΟΤΟΥΑΜΟΡΡΑΙ
ΟΥ ΚΑΙΑΠΟΤΟΥ ΥΙΩΝ
ΑΜΜΩΝΚΑΙΑΠΟ
ΦΥΛΙϹΤΙΕΙΜΚΑΙ
ΚΟΝΤΩΝΚΑΙΑΜΑ
ΛΙΚΚΑΙΜΑΔΙΑΜ
ΟΙΕΞΑΝΕΘΛΙϹΑΝΥ
ΕΚΕΚΡΑΤΕΠΡΟϹϹ
ΚΑΙΕϹΩϹΑΥΜϹ
ΧΕΙΡΟϹΑΥΤΩΝ
ΥΜΙϹΔΕΕΝΚΑ
ΤΕΛΚΑΤΕΜ
ΟΧΕΟϹΕΔΟΥ
ΛΙΧΤΟΥΤΟΟΥ
ΙϹϹΩϹΟΥ ΥΜ

ΚΑΙΟΠΟΡΕ...
...ϹΤΡΟϹ...
...ΕΔΟΟϹ...
ΚΑΤΑΥΤΟΟ...
ΟΑΝΕΥΜ...ΗΚΑ
ΙΟ ΟΥΛΟ Ν
ΚΑΙΕΠΛΑΝϹΙΥΙΟ
ΙϹΧΠΡΟϹΚΝΗΜΑ
ΤΟΜΕΝΙϹΒΟΗΘΟΝ
ΕΥΜΙΝΚΑΙΝΙΧΝ
ΤΟΛΛΑϹΟΝΕΝΟ
ΦΟΛΛΑΘΙϹϹΟΥΙϹ
...ΥΜΑϹΕΝΗ
ΗΜΕΡΑΤΑΥΤΗ
ΚΑΙΕϹΕΛΑΙΝΑΝΤ
ΘΕΟΥϹΤΟΥϹΑΛ
ΤΡΙΟΥϹΕΚΜΕϹΟΥ
ΥΤΩΝΚΑΙΕΛΟΥ
...ΝΤΩΚΩ...
...ΨΥΧΗΑΥΤΟΥΕΝΚ
ΙϹϹ...
...ΕΡΗ...Ν ΥΠ
ΘΙΑΜΜΑ...ΗΙ
ΡΕΝΕΡΑΛΟ...
ΓΑΛΑΛΑΙϹΥΜ
ΧΘΗϹΑΝ ΥΤΟ ΙϹΚΗ
ΠΑΡΕΝΕΚΛΟΝΙ
ΤΗϹΚΟΠΙΑΚΑΙΨΠΙ
ΟΛΑΟϹΟΙΑΡΧΟΝ
ΤΕϹΓΑΛΑΑΛ ΑΝΗΡ
ΠΡΟϹΤΟΝΠΛΗ
ΑΥΤΟΥΤΙϹΑΝΗΠ
ΟϹΤΙϹΑΝΑΡΞΗΤΑΙ
ΠΑΡΑΤΑΞΑϹΘΑΙ
ΠΡΟϹΤΟΥϹ ΥΙ Ν ΙΗ
ΥΙΟΥϹΑΜΜΩΝΚΑΙ
ΕϹΤΑΙϹΑϹΚΟΝΤΑ
ΠΑϹΙΝΤΟ...ΚΑΤΟΙ
ΚΟΥϹΙΝΓΑΛΑΛΑ
ΑϹΤΕΕΙϹΕΤΙΜ...
...ΕΙΤΕϹ
ΑΤΓΟϹ...ΝΟΝΤ
ΠΟΡΗ...ΟΝΕΝΗ
...
ΙΕΦΘΛΕ...ΟΤ...

Facing page:
THE LOCATION OF THE
NEW FINDS
The important collection of
manuscripts and fragments,
including one section from the
Codex Sinaiticus, was
discovered in 1975 during
building work in this area of
the monastery abutting the
northern wall close to Kleber's
Tower.

BINDING DETAILS
There are comparatively few
fine leather bindings in the
collection, but these two top
edges, one in polychrome, the
other gilt gaufrage, and their
multi-coloured headbands,
show details which emphasise
the time and expense lavished
on them.

theological use by monks for religious study, spiritual development and teaching; and their use by monks and academics from outside the community in the pursuit of historical, philosophical and theological scholarship. The location of books within the monastery in earlier centuries may well have mirrored these different functions. The gospels, psalters, service books donated to, or produced within, the monastery (for example, the austere and relatively undecorated ninth-century lectionaries and horologia probably produced at the monastery) are likely to have been stored close to the place where services were conducted, possibly the former sacristy located at the east end of the south aisle of the church. Other volumes may have been kept close to the scriptorium, or the monk's quarters, or held in repositories which could have included the room abutting the northern wall, where the important collection of pre-seventeenth century manuscript fragments was discovered in 1975 (the so-called New Finds).

Although the disposition of the collection is not known, it is clear that the manuscripts and books were at some stage dispersed, since it is recorded that the gathering together and securing of the holdings was one of the prime concerns of Archbishop Nikephoros Marthales Glykys who was at Sinai from 1728 to 1747.

The collection, cataloguing and classification was carried out by a learned and holy teacher Protosyngelos Isiah. In the nineteenth century the holdings were transferred to a new site close to the Panagia chapel, from which the flow of books could be controlled, the most valuable of them being kept in closed cabinets. This may have been in response to the removal of the Codex Sinaiticus by Constantine von Tischendorf in 1844. In 1942, under the direction of Archbishop Porphyrios III, the library was transferred to a new concrete building which gave greater security against fire and a great deal more space for the collection and for a working library. Porphyrios's successor Gregorios introduced metal bookshelves which have better preservation properties than wood. More recently,

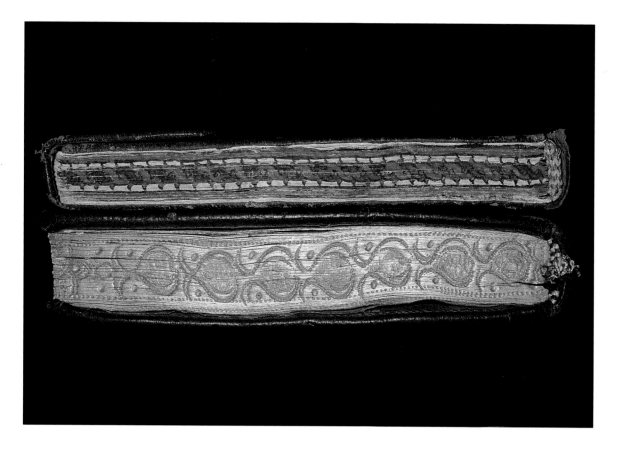

CONSERVATION OF THE
LIBRARY COLLECTION
*Manuscripts and early
printed books have bindings
in all styles, including the rich
metallic covers illustrated
earlier. Books for a more
prosaic use, are equally
interesting to the student of
bookbinding history. Many,
like the book here, employ
sewing techniques seen only in
Byzantine Middle Eastern
codices. The heavy wooden
boards and the crudely shaped
textile spine suggest that it
could have been the work of a
bookbinder, who, although he
was a skilled craftsmen,
lacked some of the materials
for his work.*

*Facing page:
The unique Library collection
presents a formidable
challenge to the conservator.
The wide range of materials
include parchment, papyrus
and Western and Arabic
paper. In many books these
have been illuminated with a
wide variety of media,
pigment-based water colours,
inks and gold leaf. This
thirteenth century
illumination of Saint Luke
gives some indication of the
need to maintain maintain
paper stability and
consolidate friable media.*

under the direction of His Eminence Archbishop Damianos and with the assistance of the National Library of Greece and the Greek Ministry of Culture, modern facilities have been installed and measures taken for the preservation of the collection and conservation of the manuscripts.

Continuity of care for the collection, and a desire to sustain scholarship, is evident throughout the known history of the monastery. The importance attached to learning, perhaps reflecting the renowned scholarship of Saint Catherine herself, and the writings of learned fathers,

42

such as Saint John Klimakos, who expressed the search for spiritual perfection in terms of ascending a ladder with thirty steps. Cataloguing, repair and rebinding is known to have been carried out in the tenth century, and at the time of Nikephoros, damaged codices and fragments were preserved by copying, harnessing the means traditionally used for dissemination. Care continues currently in the preparation of protective containers for the codices, for example, and in the use of interleaving to protect illuminated manuscripts.

The problem of the library's conservation, is in one sense

43

the general problem of all conservation, which is concerned with maintaining the identity and integrity of objects and collections for the future while allowing as far as possible, either directly or indirectly, for access and use. A juxtaposition of recent conversations at the monastery makes this duality clear: on the one hand a consideration of the environmental measures that might be taken to optimize the humidity levels in the library, ensuring the longest possible life for the codices and books; and on the other, a discussion of the various forms of scanning and information compression that might be employed to safely record their contents on CD-rom discs for widespread scholarly use. Thus, the long tradition of preserving and disseminating works through manual copying extends into the future through the application of technology.

The monks of Saint Catherine's are in this sense natural conservators. In their theological appreciation of the furniture of the world, they are attuned both to the importance of the materiality of made things and to the significance of the abstract content which transcends any particular physical embodiment. The continuing possibility of a balance between tradition and change perhaps lies in the recognition of this duality of natures.

Saint Catherine's Monastery and the Tradition of Pilgrimage

LONG BEFORE THE DISCOVERY OF SAINT CATHERINE'S mortal remains on the summit of a mountain in the Sinai Peninsula, that dramatic landscape had been the setting for pilgrimage. Moses, instructed by the angel of God from within a Burning Bush, led his people out of their oppression in Egypt, guided by a pillar of cloud by day and a pillar of fire by night. Miraculously they passed safely through the parted waters of the Red Sea, which closed again over the pursuing Egyptians. This land of Sinai was the wilderness through which the Israelites wandered for forty years, often reluctant and complaining, in search of the Promised Land.

When the Israelites lamented that the water was bitter, God showed Moses a tree with which to sweeten it. He then brought them to Elim 'where were twelve wells of water, and threescore and ten palm trees'. When in the wilderness of Sin, between Elim and Sinai, the Israelites accused Moses of rescuing them from the flesh-pots of Egypt only to allow them to die of hunger in the desert, God sent quails and manna to sustain the people. In Rephidim they grumbled again that Moses had led them there to die of thirst. At God's command Moses struck the rock in Horeb, and out flowed sweet water. These and other miraculous events ensured that this area remained sacred to three of the world's major religions. The most important happening of all took place on the top of the great mountain where God gave Moses the Law that was to be the basis of his people's way of life thereafter. Although through the centuries biblical scholars have argued about where exactly these events took place, it is now generally accepted that the imposing Mount

Spectacular views such as this from the summit of Mount Moses have evoked a varied response across the centuries, but few pilgrims can have failed to be inspired by the drama of the landscape.

47

MOSES RECEIVING THE
TABLES OF THE LAW
*This detail comes from an
early eighteenth century icon
painted in tempera. It is the
work of the painter Iacovos
Moskos and bears the
inscription 'The God-trodden
Sinai mountain'.
Monks climb the steep steps
towards the summit where
Moses can be seen stretching
out his hands to receive the
Law. Little white-walled
churches and chapels are
scattered on the lower slopes
of the mountain.*

Facing page:
THE MONASTERY OF SAINT
GALAKTION AND SAINT
EPISTEME
*The monk Galaktion and his
wife, the nun Episteme, were
martyred by Roman soldiers.
It is said that the couple fled to
Sinai during the persecutions
but they were tracked down
and met death together by
order of the Roman governor.
Their bodies were returned to
the holy mountain. This is
said to be Sinai's oldest
monastery.*

*Through the centuries
pilgrims have left the marks
of their journeys across the
mountains and valleys of
Sinai.
This view shows pathways
across Wadi ad-Dayr.*

Moses, which rises high above the Monastery of Saint Catherine, is the Mount Sinai of Exodus.

Many years after the events of Exodus, in the Roman era, when Christianity had not yet been accepted by the rulers, Christian converts fled for their lives to the Sinai Desert. Here they escaped violent death at the hands of the Romans, as there were no garrisons in the area; but they often succumbed to the hands of others, or to the privations and violence of the wilderness. There is evidence that from the

MOSES RECEIVING THE
LAW
*This icon refers to two
momentous events. Moses,
depicted as a young man, is
seen receiving the Tablets of
the Law, and at the prophet's
feet we see the cast off sandals
and the Burning Bush from
which the Lord spoke to
Moses. Around the main
image are more scenes from
the life of Moses.*

third century AD Christians banded together near the sacred sites in small communities dedicated to an ascetic way of life. From these bases they began to convert others. Thus began the earliest monastic communities.

The persecutions ceased when, in 313, the Emperor Constantine decreed that there should be freedom of worship throughout his domain. With the adoption of Christianity as the state religion, monasticism grew and spread, and so did pilgrimage. All those interested in the

history of the human spirit owe a great debt of gratitude to those early pilgrims who left a record of their thoughts and feelings as they made arduous and often very dangerous journeys to worship at the holy sites. The great drama of the origins and growth of the Monastery of Saint Catherine can be followed in the words of visitors from the time of Constantine through the heyday of pilgrimage to the Holy Land in the twelfth to the fourteenth centuries and beyond.

The earliest pilgrim to leave a detailed account is Etheria, probably a Spanish noblewoman of the fourth century. Her account of her visit to the holy sites throws considerable light on the practices of the early pilgrims, for by the time Etheria made her journey, certain customs had been established. Foremost amongst these was that of prayer. So she greeted her first sight of the holy Mount Sinai in the traditional manner. Etheria reached the foot of the mountain on the Sabbath, and she relates how she found there 'a

WADY SHO'EIB OR
JETHRO'S VALLEY

This view, taken from a print of the 1880s, is to the north-west down Wadi ad-Dayr showing the Monastery of Saint Catherine and beyond to the Plain of ar-Raaha, also known as the Plain of Assemblage where the Israelites made their camp while Moses, at God's bidding, ascended the mountain.

51

certain monastery' whose monks showed great kindness to her and her party. She says that there was also a church and a priest.

After staying overnight at the monastery, Etheria set off early the next day, accompanied by the priest and the monks, to climb to the summit of the Holy Mountain. Etheria says that it was necessary to climb 'as if up a wall' but that helped by the prayers of the holy men she achieved her goal and 'did not feel the toil' because she realised that her desire was being fulfilled 'at God's bidding'. Once at the top, she found a small chapel cared for by an old, ascetic monk. In this chapel Etheria's party, the priests and 'all the monks who dwelt on the mountain' listened to a reading from the book of Moses and then took communion.

On leaving the chapel Etheria recounts how she was given *eulogiae* (food blessed by a priest) in the form of fruits growing on the mountain. At her request the holy men proceeded to guide Etheria around the holy places. On the way down

This view of the monastery from the north east shows how vulnerable it could be from the mountain slopes above. One legend says that the man responsible for building on this site was beheaded by Justinian for his unwise choice.

Facing page:
A GLIMPSE OF THE
MONASTERY GARDEN
Good water from nearby wells make it possible for the monks and their bedouin neighbours to maintain a productive garden. Among the crops harvested are apricots, olives, tomatoes, figs and walnuts.

she was shown Elijah's cave, where the prophet hid, and here again she made earnest prayers and read biblical passages. Etheria continued in this manner, reading the appropriate texts at all the places she had desired to see, making oblations, and saying prayers. It was her intention to visit the Burning Bush, the very bush from which the angel had spoken to Moses. This she did, and once again prayers were offered. Refreshed by a meal with the holy men, and a night's sleep, Etheria visited more holy sites, meeting as she did yet more holy men.

A picture is created of a land rich with biblical associations, peppered with small monastic communities and already adapting to the growing custom of pilgrimage.

However, the church near the Burning Bush that Etheria mentions is not the building there today. One unlikely early tradition says that at the request of the monks, a church was built at the holy site by Saint Helena, the mother of the Emperor Constantine. However, a Roman emperor, the great Justinian, was certainly responsible for the present church, according to an inscription on one of the roof beams, which also establishes that the church dates from the sixth century.

Visitors today often comment on the slightly odd orientation of the monastery's walls and on its vulnerability to occasional flooding and to attack from above. If, as tradition suggests, Justinian built the monastery not only for the protection of the monks so that they could continue with their spiritual vocation, but also to provide the Roman Empire with a strategically placed fortress, then why is its location so far from perfect? The answer probably lies in the supreme importance attached to the little piece of land where Moses was told in Exodus, 3:5, 'Put off thy shoes from off thy feet, for the place whereon thou standest is holy ground', when he stood in awe before the bush that burned with fire but was not consumed. A plan of the current monastery reveals how the bush grows in the lowest corner of the rectangle formed by the walls, the area most liable to flooding.

Facing page:
INTERIOR OF THE
CHURCH OF THE
TRANSFIGURATION
looking eastwards towards the iconostasis. The mosaic of the Transfiguration in the apse, from which the church takes its name, is obscured in this view by the splendid chandeliers. Icons which are attached to the great pillars of the nave can be seen.

In Justinian's time, as in Etheria's, the bush grew outside the church walls. Pilgrims visiting this holy site in the years after Justinian's building programme would probably have entered the church through a door opening onto one of the side aisles. They would have walked the length of the building, possibly visiting chapels on the way, before entering the courtyard at the east end where the Burning Bush grew. However, by the early thirteenth century, a roofed chapel occupied the site, its altar marking the exact spot where the bush had stood. At least one pilgrim said that the bush had all been taken away by souvenir-seeking pilgrims.

THE CHAPEL OF
SAINT CATHERINE ON
THE SUMMIT OF
JEBEL KATARINA
*This chapel was built on the
highest peak in the range,
where the body of Saint
Catherine was found. Over
many years pilgrims made the
long and hazardous ascent to
see the spot on which the saint
was set down by angels. Much
later, her body was brought
down to the monastery and
encased in a tomb in the
church where it continued to
attract countless pilgrims.*

But tradition says that when the chapel was built to protect that most holy of sites, the bush itself was transplanted just a short distance away, so that it could flourish in God's daylight. It flourishes still, and pilgrims sometimes carry away cuttings, gifts from the monks, as mementos of their pilgrimage. A little sprig of leaves from the Burning Bush is just one of the many souvenirs of pilgrimage that have been sought by the pious and the not so pious across the centuries.

The fortunes of the Monastery of Saint Catherine have been inextricably linked with the tradition of the most valuable and precious type of souvenir, the holy relic. A relic is something that has been closely associated with a holy person during their lifetime, an article of clothing or of daily use, perhaps, or an object connected with the holy person's death, their body, or a bodily part. The miracle-working properties attributed to relics have made them a valuable spiritual commodity.

Previous page:
THE RELICS OF SAINT
CATHERINE BEING
CARRIED IN PROCESSION
ON HER FEAST DAY IN
1995
*The precious caskets, carried
by the archbishop and a
visiting bishop, contain all
that remains of the body of
Saint Catherine at the
monastery: part of her skull
and her left hand. Over the
centuries other precious relics
of the saint have come to rest
in other countries.
Souvenir-hunting pilgrims
and other less spiritual
visitors have also taken a
heavy toll of the treasures of
the monastery.*

The Monastery of Saint Catherine, originally dedicated to the Virgin, received its current name after the remains of Saint Catherine of Alexandria were discovered at the peak of the mountain now associated with the young, wise and beautiful woman martyred for her unshakeable Christian faith in the early fourth century. *The Golden Legend,* a late thirteenth century compilation of edifying stories about the lives of the saints and, after the Bible, perhaps the most widely read book during the late Middle Ages, relates that after the Roman emperor had tried unsuccessfully to break her body and her spirit on a spiked wheel, he had Saint Catherine beheaded. Immediately on her death her body was taken by angels to Mount Sinai, so the legend continues, and a miraculous oil flowed from her bones thereafter. Monastic teaching links the place where the body was found with the peak now called Mount Catherine. It is said that as she died she promised that those who remembered her would be blessed. A special chapel was built in her honour on the top of the mountain, and monks climbed that imposing peak to say mass there until at least 1096.

A strange event caused the cult of Saint Catherine to spread widely. It was the custom to collect some of the holy oil exuded by the bones of the holy woman. On one of these occasions one of the saint's fingers broke off and fell into the reliquary. The monk involved took these precious relics with him as he journeyed in Europe seeking funds to help the monastery. The relics finally came to rest in the

THE FOURTEEN
AUXILIARY SAINTS
These are two Northern European single sheet woodcuts showing the saints to whom people prayed for help with bodily ailments ranging from toothache to the plague. The first group is divided in the centre by the Crucifixion with the Virgin and Saint John. Third from the right in the second image is Saint Catherine with sword and wheel.

Facing page:
SAINT CATHERINE
OF ALEXANDRIA
The many surviving woodcuts with an image of Saint Catherine testify to her enormous popularity in the west. Many institutions were dedicated to her.
In this hand-coloured woodcut she is shown with her attributes, the sword and the wheel.

abbey church in Rouen, where they began to work miracles, spreading the fame of Saint Catherine. One tradition suggests that some time after 1096 the bones of the saint were brought down from the mountain and laid to rest in the chapel dedicated to Saint Catherine within the church.

Travellers journeyed in increasing numbers to the shrine of Saint Catherine, although not all of them had purely spiritual motives for doing so. Some used the pretence of pilgrimage to spy on the military strength of the Muslim kingdoms. After the Islamic conquests, which left the monastery unscathed and largely unaffected, Crusader

THE CHURCH OF THE HOLY TRINITY *on the summit of Mount Sinai (Jebel Musa) where Moses received the tablets of the Law. The present building was erected in 1934 partly from materials remaining from the sixth century church. The peak has been the goal of pilgrims for many centuries.*

Loaves baked at Saint Catherine's for use in the church services are decorated by being impressed with wooden stamps showing a variety of images, including the Burning Bush, the Monastery and the figure of Saint Catherine.

Previous page:
THE STAIRWAY OF
REPENTANCE
leading to the summit of Jebel Musa. The archway is known as the Shrive Gate of Saint Stephen because it was here in the sixth century that an aged Holy Man tested pilgrim's piety before allowing them to continue their ascent. It is said that this archway was built by Moses and another further up the mountain by the prophet Elijah.
Saint Stephen, wearing a robe of the highest monastic rank, rests to this day in the charnel house of the monastery.

64

pilgrims often visited the monastery to gain the one year's indulgence (remission of time spent in purgatory for earthly sins) granted by the pope.

From the twelfth to the fourteenth centuries a veritable tourist industry developed, surrounded by much of the paraphernalia familiar to the twentieth century. Guidebooks were written giving routes and itineraries, advice on lodgings, types of transport, food and medicines and even useful foreign phrases. An increasing number of Europeans included Saint Catherine's in their Holy Land itineraries. While many of these intrepid travellers were

ИЗОБРАЖЕНІЕ СВ. ГОРЫ СИНАЙСКОЙ И МОНАСТЫРЯ СВ ВЕЛИКОМУЧЕНИЦЫ ЕКАТЕРИНЫ

genuine pilgrims, others were motivated by a desire to visit a strange and exotic land. Still others came to Saint Catherine's in search of healing, for it had long been believed that the relics of a saint had the power to protect and to heal.

The Golden Legend speaks of an oil that issued continuously from Saint Catherine's bones, mending the limbs of all who were weak. Frescobaldi, a devout Tuscan nobleman, visited the monastery in 1384, describes how he was given a small phial of the miracle-working 'white manna' that flowed from the ears of Saint Catherine. Frescobaldi was probably typical of many pious visitors who toiled round the sacred sites in the fourteenth century. He speaks with gratitude of the monks, their hospitality and willingness to act as holy guides on arduous treks up dangerous mountain paths. As Frescobaldi endeavours to gain the indulgence

This lithograph of 1872 shows Russian pilgrims at the Monastery of Saint Catherine.

Directly behind the buildings looms the majestic peak of Jebel Musa. To the left is Jebel ad-Dayr and to the right Jebel Katarina.

During the nineteenth century countless Russian pilgrims visited the monastery and many treasures of Russian origin are to be found within its walls.

MEMENTOS OF
PILGRIMAGE
*A small group of objects sold
to the late twentieth century
visitor at the Monastery of
Saint Catherine or nearby.
Such simple tokens of
journeys successfully made
have been offered to pilgrims in
many different forms across
the years.*

granted by climbing to the summit of Mount Sinai, he tells the stories associated with the different sites and comments on the degrees of danger and difficulty presented by the terrain. At the summit of Mount Catherine he uses a chisel especially brought for the purpose to chip away at the rock on which the angels deposited the body of Saint Catherine. He manages at last to break off some stone, 'which they say is a good cure for fever'. Signor Gucci, a fellow traveller, laboured similarly to the top of Mount Sinai, taking for a reward a few splinters from the rock on which Moses stood to receive the Ten Commandments. Such holy fragments were much prized back in Europe. It is not hard to see how such pious vandalism, however well-intentioned, could lead to serious problems.

Like so many others Frescobaldi was not only in the Sinai for the good of his soul but also as a keen observer able to gather information about the terrain that would have a military value for European rulers. Early in the fifteenth century the number of pilgrims dropped as the Turkish threat to Byzantium grew, and in 1453 Constantinople finally fell to the Ottomans. However, after 1460 the flow of pilgrims increased once more, and in 1483 a vigorous Swiss-born Dominican from Ulm, Friar Felix Fabri, added his account to the many already in existence. This holy man had become a friar on the very feast day of Saint Catherine (25 November) in 1453 and was fulfilling a long-standing desire to visit her shrine. That souvenir-hunting had in no way lessened in the century since Frescobaldi and his party had visited Saint Catherine's is indicated by an incident described by Felix Fabri: his party's departure from the monastery was delayed until one of its members had returned a fragment that he had broken from the reliquary containing Saint Catherine's remains.

The lively comments of Brother Felix, religious pilgrim though he was, reflect in many ways the attitudes and practices of the twentieth-century tourist. Certainly the friar had a good eye for a souvenir. He gathered into his basket anything that took his eye as he travelled, including a bitter fruit that tainted the rest of his supplies and the 'prettiest pebbles', transparent and shining with different colours.

The good man suffered, as travellers always have, from anxieties about the security of his possessions. It was the custom for pilgrims to carry with them rings and other valuables belonging to friends and patrons back home who were unable or unwilling to make the journey themselves. These articles were believed to be imbued with sanctity and curative powers by being placed in contact with the bones of the saint. So although the friar probably carried few riches of his own, he had the jewels of others to concern him. By Felix Fabri's time, in fact, professionals could be hired to make a pilgrimage on behalf of a patron.

Even before Felix Fabri made his long-desired visit to Mount Sinai and the Monastery of Saint Catherine, a complex state of affairs existed. Many and various were the motives for the journey, and equally varied were the attitudes and responses to the experiences gained. This continued to

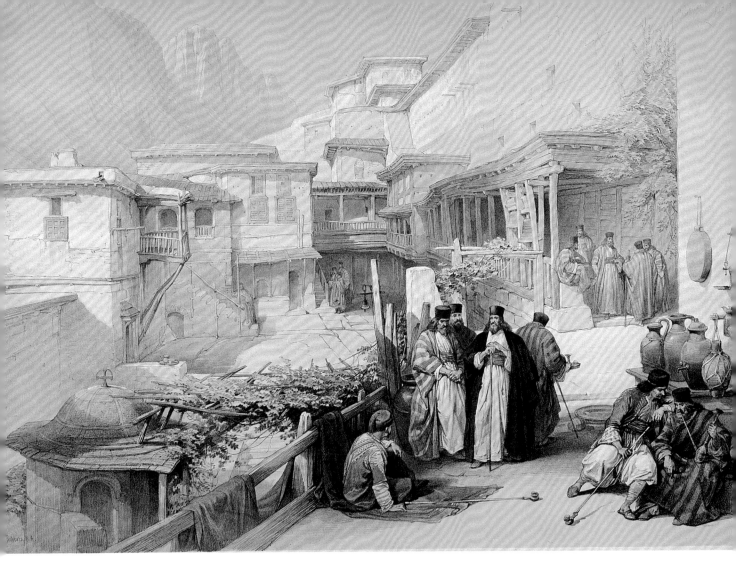

be true through succeeding centuries and remains so still.

As travel is made easier the problems increase for Saint Catherine's small community of monks, endeavouring to fulfil their spiritual work. There have always been, and will always be, difficulties in dealing with the complexities of the human spirit. Perhaps each potential visitor should consider carefully their reasons for seeking the sacred places of Saint Catherine's, and reflect on the words of Santo Brasca who made a pilgrimage to the Holy Land in 1480: 'Let no man go ... just to see the world or that he may boast "I've been there, I've seen that" and so impress his friends'.

David Roberts

Justinian's Fortified Monastery

CYRIL MANGO

A BIBLICAL HOLY PLACE, A CENTRE OF PILGRIMAGE, A monastery and a fortress: Saint Catherine's, as it came to be called in the later Middle Ages, has for many centuries combined these different functions. How it all started we do not know. The books of Exodus and Numbers, in describing the life of Moses and the wanderings of the children of Israel on their way from Egypt to the Promised Land, refer to a number of places leading up to the 'Mountain of God', called Horeb or Sinai, the latter (assuming they were one and the same) being situated in the land of Midian. It was there that Moses tended the flocks of Jethro, his father-in-law, and saw the vision of the Burning Bush; there, too, Moses led his people after they had crossed the Red Sea. On the summit of Sinai, covered by a dark cloud, God spoke to Moses and handed him the tablets of the Law.

It may be that already in pre-Christian times there existed a tradition as to where these various places were situated, and that when the great movement of Christian monasticism developed in the third and fourth centuries AD, groups of anchorites made their way to the Sinai Peninsula not only because it was a wilderness, but also on account of its rich biblical associations. Yet there is no clear evidence that the Jews had any firm tradition on that score. It is equally possible, therefore, that it was the Christian monks (there being at first no other Christians on Sinai) who worked out the biblical topography and made the identifications that were to become canonical

Our first fixed point is provided by the visit to Sinai of Etheria, a rich lady from Gaul or Spain, in AD 383. By

THE MONASTERY OF SAINT CATHERINE *is the best preserved holy site of the early Christian period. However, this view reveals the vulnerability of its location in a narrow valley overlooked by mountains.*

Facing page:
The granite walls have
endured raids and
earthquakes and though
patched-up in places still
stand to their full height.

that time an organized pilgrimage route had already been established and every place of biblical interest exactly localized. Etheria climbed Mount Sinai (the present Jebel Musa) on foot — it took her four hours — and, with her usual thoroughness, performed her devotions at each and every holy spot in the vicinity: the chapel on the summit and, next to it, the cave in which Moses had stood; another cave further down in which the prophet Elijah hid when he had fled from Jezebel; the spot at the foot of the mountain where Aaron had stood with the seventy elders and, of course, the Burning Bush, which was still flourishing. There was a garden with excellent water, a church and many hermitages round about, but as yet no central monastery. Etheria does not intimate that the many monks she met on the peninsula (some of whom acted as guides) were in any danger from nomadic Arabs.

Numberless other pilgrims followed in Etheria's footsteps. Some took the shorter route from Palestine across the Negev Desert; others, like Etheria, travelled along the west coast of the peninsula and were offered the extra bonus of visiting Clysma (Suez), where the tracks of Pharaoh's chariots were still visible. They stopped at Marah, with its bitter waters, and Elim, with its twelve wells and seventy palm trees, a prefiguration of the twelve apostles and seventy disciples of Christ. Visitors from all parts of the Christian world had to be accommodated for shorter or longer periods. They also needed interpreters, fluent not only in Greek and Latin, but also in Coptic and Syriac, Armenian and Georgian and even Bessic (a now-extinct Thracian language).

It seems, however, that conditions on Sinai were gradually becoming less secure, and it was this circumstance that must have impelled the Emperor Justinian to build the fortified monastery that still exists today. In all parts of his far-flung empire, but especially along its eastern borders, Justinian went to extraordinary lengths to erect defensive works in a vain attempt to keep his enemies at bay. His building activity was recorded in a special work of circa 554

entitled *Peri ktismaton*. It was composed by the historian
Procopius of Caesarea, who happens to be in this connection our only contemporary witness. His actual words are
worth quoting:

> An abrupt and terribly desolate mountain, Sinai by name,
> rises very close to the Red Sea . . . On this Mount Sinai
> there live monks, whose life is a close study of death,
> and they enjoy without fear the solitude that is so dear
> to them. Since there was nothing they desired — indeed,
> they are superior to all things human and do not seek to
> own anything or care for their bodies or have enjoyment
> of anything else — the Emperor Justinian built for these
> monks a church, which he dedicated to the Mother of
> God, so they might be able to dwell there praying and

73

performing their holy rites. This church he built not on
the summit of the mountain, but much lower down, for
it is impossible for a man to remain overnight on the
summit, seeing that constant crashes and other divine
manifestations are heard there at night, terrifying human
strength and mind. In that place they say that Moses
received the laws from God and made them public. At
the foot of the mountain the emperor also built a very
strong fortress and made it an important military strong-
hold so that the barbarian Saracens might not be able to
penetrate from there by stealth — the region being un-
inhabited — into the lands of Palestine.

This passage raises one difficulty. It seems to suggest that
the Church of the Mother of God, built for the monks
already established in those inhospitable parts, was
distinct from the fortress in which a body of troops was
stationed — not for the protection of the monks, but

for the purely strategic purpose of checking the inroads of nomadic Arabs into Palestine. Procopius was himself a Palestinian, but there is no reason to suppose that he ever went to Sinai, and he may have got some details wrong. On the other hand, he certainly had access to government sources, so that the strategic motivation he mentions was probably based on good authority. If so, we may view the construction of the fortified monastery not so much as an act of pure piety, but as part of Justinian's overarching military design.

Several centuries later, when the realities of Justinian's reign had been forgotten and legend had had time to weave its web, a different account was given. It is preserved by Eutychius, Patriarch of Alexandria, who lived in the tenth century and wrote in Arabic. Here it is the monks of Sinai, still living in dispersed hermitages and having for protection nothing but a tower near the Burning Bush, who petition the emperor for a secure monastery. Justinian sends an emissary who, after consideration, rejects the option of building a monastery on the summit of the mountain (there being no water there) and establishes it instead at the tower, which is preserved within the new enclosure. Placed in a narrow valley, the monastery is, however, directly overlooked by the mountain to the north, hence insecure. When the emissary returns to Constantinople to give an account of his actions, Justinian is angered by the unsatisfactory solution he has adopted and orders his head to be cut off. To remedy the weakness of the monastery, he despatches two hundred slaves with their wives and children to Sinai. They are to act as a permanent guard, and special quarters are built for them outside the monastery, to the east. A century later, when the Arabs occupy Sinai, the descendants of the slaves embrace Islam. The monks destroy their quarters, which, adds Eutychius, remain as ruins to his day. It is an attractive story, which may even contain some genuine information, such as the references to the tower and the ruined quarters of the guards.

Built of squared blocks of local granite, Justinian's

Facing page:
The church surrounded by a cluster of monastic buildings. Within the monastery's walls the narrow alleyways and small courts convey the impression of a small ancient town.

75

monastery has miraculously survived and is, indeed, better preserved than any other holy site of the early Christian period. The walls, though patched-up in places, still stand to their full height. In plan they form a trapezoid of about ninety by seventy-five metres, without real towers, hence not a very sophisticated piece of military architecture, but, no doubt, considered adequate to deter nomadic tribesmen. Over the original door (now blocked) one may dimly see the inscription, 'This is the gate of the Lord, through which the righteous shall enter. [Work] of the Emperor Justinian, lover of Christ'. Inside, the chief monument is the church, a three-aisled, timber-roofed basilica with lateral chapels. Its position, not centred or properly aligned with regard to the enclosure, must have been determined by that of the Burning Bush, originally displayed in an open courtyard behind the apse. Wishing to keep the bush and the nave on the same level the architect was also obliged to cut the church into the sloping ground, so that one goes down to its porch by a staircase. As befits a monastery, the church is rather simple. The capitals of its twelve columns, each one exhibiting a different pattern, are rather crudely executed. The original roof beams are still in place, carved on the underside with a variety of animal and vegetal motifs and bearing three important inscriptions petitioning God to guard the pious Emperor Justinian; to grant repose to the deceased Empress Theodora; and to have mercy on the master-builder Stephen of Aila and his children. The inscriptions help us determine the date of the church: after the death of Theodora (548) and before that of Justinian (565). Seeing, however, that the church had been built when Procopius was writing his treatise (circa 554), we may assign it to circa 550.

An inscription on one of the three inscribed ceiling beams in the church. The inscriptions with their references to the Byzantine Emperor Justinian, his Empress Theodora and the architect Stephen of Aila, taken with other evidence, allow a precise dating of the building.

Facing page:
THE BELLTOWER AND
THE WESTERN END OF
THE CHURCH
The church and its surrounding buildings emphasise the sloping ground on which the monastery is built.

77

THE PRESBYTER
LONGINUS
*The mosaic of the
Transfiguration was made in
the latter part of the sixth
century when Longinus was
Abbot of Saint Catherine's
Monastery.*

It was highly unusual at the time for an architect to sign his own work. Stephen of Aila ('Aqaba) was a local man, a native of the nearest big settlement, and none too literate, judging by the inscription in his name, which is garbled and barely intelligible. In other words, no need was felt to import a fancy architect from a great metropolis. Stephen did an honest job which has stood the test of time.

In contrast to the simplicity of the architecture, the great mosaic at the east end of the church strikes us by the rich subtlety of its execution and the complexity of its theological message. It also happens to be perfectly preserved and almost untouched by later restoration. There has been a great deal of discussion among scholars about its date, which depends on the interpretation of the inscription placed at the base of the apse:

> In the name of the Father, the Son and the Holy Spirit, this entire work was done for the salvation of the donors at the time of the most reverend Longinus, presbyter and abbot, by the solicitude of Theodore, presbyter and second-in-command. Indiction 14.

MOSES LOOSENING HIS
SANDAL BEFORE THE
BURNING BUSH
*This mosaic occupies the upper
part of the eastern wall of the
sanctuary of the church,
above the Triumphal Arch.*

Longinus happens to be unknown. As to the indictional date,
it tells us merely that the work was carried out in the fourteenth year of any successive fifteen-year assessment cycle
excluding 550-51, when the abbot was called George. The
date could have been 565-66 (the Byzantine year start-
ing on 1 September), 580-81, 595-96, or even later, but most
probably before the political upheavals of the seventh
century, which isolated Sinai from the Byzantine world. The
inscription tells us something else: the execution of the
mosaic was not carried out under imperial auspices. It
was a local effort, financed by private donors and taken in
hand by the aforementioned Theodore. At either end of the

79

inscription are the portraits of two contemporary clerics, distinguished by their lifelike features and their square 'haloes' (a convention which indicated that the person depicted was still alive): on the right the Abbot Longinus, blue-eyed and heavy jowled; on the left, not, as we might have expected, Theodore, but a certain Deacon John, whose identity remains unknown. Was he perhaps the principal donor?

The mosaic at the eastern end of the church represents two scenes of local relevance: Moses loosening his sandals in front of the Burning Bush, and Moses receiving the tablets of the Law from the hand of God. These scenes are placed very high up, whereas the principal composition in the apse, to which the worshipper's gaze was immediately directed before the insertion of the present high iconostasis, represents the Transfiguration of Christ, an event that took place on another mountain, that of Tabor in Galilee. Why the Transfiguration? Because it was seen as the fulfilment of Moses' incomplete vision. On Sinai Moses did not see God face to face; on Tabor he, Elijah and the three chosen apostles were able to see Christ in His divine glory. On Sinai there was a dark cloud, on Tabor a luminous one. On Horeb Moses said (in the King James version), 'I will now turn aside and see this great sight', which in the Greek of the Septuagint reads, 'Parelthon opsomai to horama to mega touto'. *Parelthon* means literally 'having gone by'. What did he mean by that? He meant 'after I have traversed my earthly life, after the period of the Law has gone by'. Only then will the great sight of the New Dispensation be revealed on Mount Tabor, and Moses will be there to see it. Furthermore, the Transfiguration was only made known after the Resurrection, for Christ said (Matthew 17.9), 'Tell the vision *(to horama)* to no man, until the Son of Man be risen again from the dead'. The complementarity of Sinai and Tabor is explained at length in a sermon on the Transfiguration by Anastasius the Sinaite.

The Sinai mosaic may be read to reveal further layers of meaning. Moses, for example, is shown growing older in age in each of the three scenes in which he appears. He is in his prime before the Burning Bush, grizzled when he receives the tablets of the Law and very old in the Transfiguration. True to Anastasius's formulation, he has 'traversed' his life before being deemed worthy of the divine vision. Elijah, whose very cave was above the monastery, wears not only his traditional mantle of sheepskin, but also a thin black belt decorated with white crosslets, the kind of belt worn by Christian monks. He represents, therefore, the archetypal monk, Christian by anticipation, and indicates that the monk, like himself, may attain to the sight of God. Rather more difficult to explain, but surely intentional, is another feature that may strike us as odd.

Facing page:
THE ICONOSTASIS OF
THE CHURCH OF THE
TRANSFIGURATION
This partition separating the nave from the sanctuary is similar to the chancel screen of the western church. In the Eastern Orthodox church it is used to display icons in a fixed order. This gilded iconostasis came from Crete and was built in 1612.

81

Unlike later Byzantine representations of the Transfiguration, which always depict a craggy mountaintop, the Sinai mosaic omits the physical setting. There is only a horizontal strip of ground, shading off from dark green to yellow as it is illuminated by Christ's radiance. While Elijah and Moses stand securely upon this strip, the three frightened apostles appear to levitate. The kneeling posture of John and James, and Peter's prostrate figure, require more solid support. We may imagine that the model the artist was following included the summit of Tabor. Did he leave it out to make the scene more timeless and less specific?

Justinian's monastery enjoyed less than a century of peace, during which time it manifested a remarkable flowering under two distinguished abbots, Saint John Klimakos, author of the *Spiritual Ladder,* the classic guide to monastic perfection, and Anastasius the Sinaite, a prolific author of theological literature. A notable visitor was John Moschus, author of the *Spiritual Meadow,* who died in Rome but wished to be buried on Sinai. When, however, his body had been conveyed to the East in 634, the route to the Holy Mountain proved too hazardous. We have only one descriptive account of Sinai after Justinian's intervention, from that of an anonymous pilgrim from Piacenza in Italy (circa 570). He comments on the wildlife of the surrounding countryside (lions, leopards, wild asses and goats, all living together in harmony), on the dew or manna that collected in the valley and coagulated into a kind of mastic, which was added to water to produce an infusion, and on an Arab idol on Mount Horeb, made of white marble, which turned black every new moon.

We do not know how the monastery coped, first, with the instability that prevailed in the seventh century, and then, with the Arab conquest. It certainly lost its treasure, the liturgical silver comprising patens, chalices, lamps and so on, that must have been offered to it in its early days. Today only one bronze cross of sixth-century date survives. There is no medieval treasure either. Books and wooden icons were of less interest to looters. Somehow the monastery survived and maintained its pan-Christian character, including as it did not only Greek-speaking monks, but also Georgians, Christian Arabs and other nationalities. The present composition of the library reflects this mixture: while two-thirds of the extant four thousand manuscripts are in Greek, the remainder are in Arabic, Syriac, Georgian, Slavonic and Ethiopic. The monastery forged links not only with the Byzantine Empire, but also with the papacy and the Latin West. By the thirteenth century it held estates and other assets at Cairo, Faran, Alexandria, Petra, Jerusalem, Acre, Damascus, Laodicea, Antioch, Constantinople, Crete and Cyprus.

The acquisition of the body of Saint Catherine, which is shrouded in complete mystery, provided a further inducement to help from the West, where that particular saint was held in great esteem.

The treasures of the monastery fall into two main categories: icons and manuscripts. Saint Catherine's has by far the most important collection of icons in the world — Byzantine, Crusader and post-Byzantine, ranging in date from the sixth century to the present day. It also holds, as we have said, over four thousand manuscripts covering a similar time-span, as well as an important collection of charters and other documents. Only when this material has been systematically studied will it be possible to write in full the history of the monastery, which reflects the tribulations of eastern Christianity over a millennium and a half.

A Venerable Manuscript Collection

SEBASTIAN BROCK

THE MONASTERY LIBRARY OF SAINT CATHERINE'S houses one of the finest collections of manuscripts in the world—over four thousand codices and scrolls in eleven different languages, reflecting the varied linguistic backgrounds of the monks, and of visitors, over the ages. About two-thirds of the manuscripts are written in Greek—the Monastery became predominantly Greek-speaking in the sixteenth century—while the remainder for the most part consists of significant holdings in Syriac, Christian Palestinian Aramaic, Georgian, Arabic and Slavonic. Not surprisingly, the texts copied were mainly biblical and liturgical books; various writings of the Church Fathers are naturally well represented, but there is also a small number of secular texts, including a few classical authors.

Several manuscripts provide details of the date and place of writing, and from these, and other indications, something of the history of the collection can be traced. A large number of manuscripts, including most of the finest pieces in the collection, were acquired through presentation to the monastery. The earliest recorded donation dates from AD 837. The manuscript, now alas divided up among many different libraries, contains the *Book of Perfection* by the early seventh-century Syriac writer Martyrius, and was written in Edessa (Urfa). The scribe has himself added that he had donated it to 'the shrine of Saint Moses on the holy mountain of Sinai'. From the second half of the ninth century there survive three manuscripts, one in Georgian (of 864), and two in Arabic (of 885-86), which were copied in the famous Palestinian monastery of Mar Saba

Facing page:
SAINT GREGORY OF NAZIANUS
This page from the Homilies of Gregory of Nazianzus (Greek ms 339) shows Saint Gregory beginning to compose his sermons. The manuscript was written between 1136 and 1155 in Constantinople. The complex image depicted here serves as a frontispiece to the book, and shows an ornamental setting with elements derived from real architecture.

85

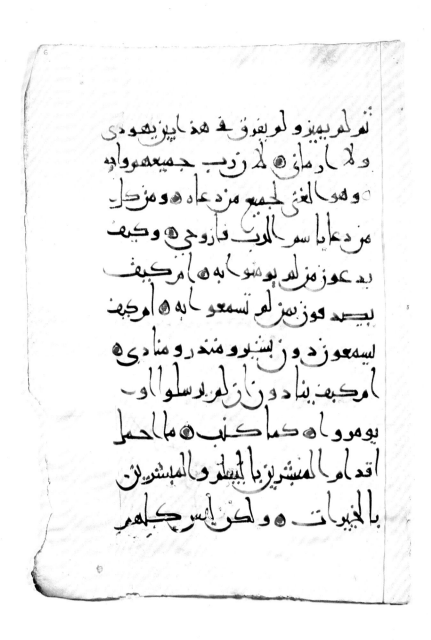

specifically for the monastery on Mount Sinai.

Many other manuscripts, above all those with monastic or liturgical texts, were copied at the monastery itself. The earliest manuscripts definitely known to have been written on Sinai are two collections of martyrdoms, one in Arabic, dated 868, and the other in Syriac, dated 886. The colophons of a number of late tenth-century manuscripts also specifically state that they were written in the monastery; the majority of these are in Georgian (dated to 974, 977, 978, 979 and 981 or 983). A bilingual text of the Gospels, in Greek and Arabic, dated to 995 or 996, is the earliest

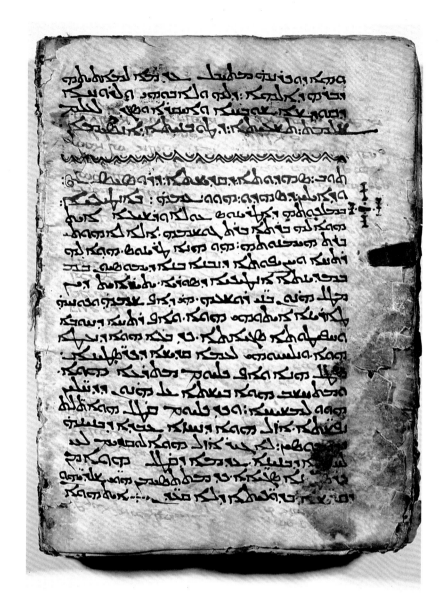

Greek manuscript known to have been written on Sinai. These early dated manuscripts give an excellent indication of the multilingual character of Saint Catherine's in the ninth and tenth centuries. Another period of considerable scribal activity in the monastery seems to have been the twelfth and thirteenth centuries, for many dated manuscripts in a variety of languages belong to this time. Among the later Greek manuscripts, it is interesting to learn that a small number were copied by women.

The manuscripts are written on papyrus, parchment and paper (the monastery happens to possess one of the

88

oldest known Greek manuscripts written on oriental paper, the Greek-Arabic Gospel lectionary of 995 or 996, mentioned above). The vast majority of manuscripts are in codex, or book, form, but the collection also includes a considerable number of liturgical scrolls. There is, furthermore, a large archive of documents, among which the Arabic and Turkish firmans from the medieval and Ottoman periods are especially important.

In 1975, in the course of restoration work, a blocked-up room containing a large number of manuscripts was discovered. Like the old collection, these 'New Finds' are in Greek and a variety of other languages, including Arabic, Georgian, Slavonic and Syriac. The New Finds, which include manuscripts and fragments of great antiquity, add very significantly to the importance of the Saint Catherine's manuscript collection.

The earliest catalogue of the monastery's holdings is a tenth-century Georgian manuscript which classifies some fifty Georgian manuscripts under twenty-two categories. One particular Georgian scribe from this period, John Zosimos, is known to have restored and rebound a number of volumes himself. The beginnings of a catalogue of the Greek collection go back to 1704. A classification system was introduced in 1734 by Archbishop Nikephoros Marthalis. In the course of the second half of the nineteenth century, basic catalogues of many of the collections were produced, and more detailed ones of certain categories of manuscript (notably the illuminated Greek texts) have been published more recently. Through the initiative of Archbishop Damianos and the Iera Synaxis of the monastery, catalogues of the important New Finds are in the process of being prepared, and some have already been published. Thanks to Archbishop Porphyrios III, the present library wing was completed in 1942.

Pride of place among the Greek manuscripts must undoubtedly be accorded to the Codex Sinaiticus par excellence, one of the most important manuscripts of the Greek Bible, dating from the fourth century. From the monastery's

SAINT JOHN KLIMAKOS
OFFERS HIS BOOK TO
CHRIST
*from a twelfth-century copy
(Greek ms 418) of the
'Spiritual Ladder', probably
written and illustrated in
Sinai. This dedication picture
is unique among surviving
copies of the 'Ladder'. Abbot
Saint John Klimakos wrote
his famous text formulating
the spiritual exercise of the
monastic community during
the seventh century.*

point of view this precious treasure has had a sad history: in 1859 the great biblical scholar Constantine vonn Tischendorf, on one of his several visits to the monastery, borrowed the manuscript in order to show it to Tsar Alexander II. Instead of returning it to Saint Catherine's, he presented the manuscript to the tsar in 1862, together with a magnificent four-volume facsimile edition.

Subsequently, thanks to considerable pressure from the Russian authorities, the 'donation' was regularized by Archbishop Kallistratos. The manuscript changed hands again in 1933, when it was sold by the Soviet Union to the British Museum, where it is now on permanent display. Though robbed of the greater part of its finest treasure, the monastery still retains thirteen folios from near the beginning of the manuscript, but it was only in 1975 that these came to light, among the New Finds.

Not surprisingly, the vast majority of the Greek manuscripts contain biblical, liturgical and patristic texts; these last include not only the great Greek Fathers of the early Church, such as Saint John Chrysostom and Saint Gregory of Nazianzus, but also many later writers like Saint John of Sinai (better known as Saint John Klimakos, 'of the *Ladder*') and Saint John of Damascus. Monastic texts, which are naturally very well represented, include translations from the Syriac Fathers, Saint Ephrem and Saint Isaac the Syrian. Many of these manuscripts are also wonderful examples of Greek calligraphy, in both the majuscule (uncial) and minuscule scripts.

The number of secular texts is rather small, but of particular importance among them is a ninth-century manuscript, from the New Finds, containing Books i-v of Homer's *Iliad*, accompanied by a paraphrase.

Quite a number of the Greek manuscripts are illustrated. The finest of these, dating from the eleventh and twelfth centuries, were probably originally produced in Constantinople, but were subsequently donated to the monastery. An eleventh-century copy of the Book of Job (Greek ms 3) is provided with a particularly splendid set of twenty-seven illustrations, among which is one of Job's wife dutifully providing her husband with food. She is shown presenting the plate perched on the end of a long pole, due to the stink of the dungheap upon which the afflicted man is seated. Lectionaries were frequently singled out for illustration, and one such manuscript of circa AD1000 (Greek ms 204) has exceptionally fine full-standing portraits of the Evangelists, Christ and the Virgin Mary set against a gold ground. Another manuscript of Constantinopolitan origin contains Saint John Chrysostom's Homilies on Matthew (Greek ms 364), but is also provided with portraits of the Emperor Constantine ix Monomachos (1042-50), his wife the Empress Zoe and her sister Theodora. The illustrator of a

*Here we see the long-suffering
Job sitting naked upon the
dung hill being offered food by
his wife, who keeps a safe
distance away from the
stinking heap and her
husband's afflicted body. This
image comes from an eleventh-
century Book of Job made in
Constantinople. (Greek ms
3, fol. 26r) The Book of Job,
a book of suffering and
contemplation, was a
favourite text of the
Byzantines.*

further patristic manuscript (Greek ms 339), besides providing appropriate scenes to illustrate a liturgical collection of the Homilies of Saint Gregory of Nazianzus, has enjoyed himself by decorating many letters with flute-playing monkeys and other such animals.

It is possible that, among the many manuscripts copied in the monastery itself during the eleventh, twelfth and thirteenth centuries, two remarkable illustrated manuscripts should be included, one of the eleventh century (Greek ms 1186) containing the *Christian Topography* by the sixth-century writer Kosmas Indikopleustes ('sailor on the Indian Ocean'), and the other of the twelfth century (Greek ms 418) with the famous monastic work, the *Spiritual Ladder*, by Saint John of Sinai (Saint John Klimakos). In the latter manuscript, in an illustration accompanying Chapter 19 of the *Ladder*, on 'Sleep, Prayer and Psalmody', we see a monk variously depicted singing psalms, at prayer, and in bed: the monk who is cosily tucked up for the night, however, has a black devil flying dangerously above his head!

The substantial collections of manuscripts in Syriac, Arabic, Georgian, Christian Palestinian Aramaic and Slavonic are all of great interest, for a variety of different reasons. Connections between Syriac-speaking monks and Sinai go

back to the fourth century AD, and it is to the fourth or fifth century that the oldest and most important Syriac manuscript belongs: often referred to as the Sinaiticus Syriacus par excellence, it is a palimpsest in which the underwriting contains the earliest translation of the Gospels into Syriac, for which only one other manuscript is known. The Syriac collection also includes a number of important translations of Greek writers (including a few pagan ones, such as Lucian and Plutarch). Two deserve special mention: Syriac ms 10 preserves the sole complete text of the *Apology* of Aristeides (second century), a work whose Greek original is only known through its having been adapted for use in the *History of Barlaam and Josaphat*, attributed to Saint John of Damascus. The true author of the extremely influential collection of texts put out under the name of Dionysius the Areopagite at the end of the fifth

A CHRISTIAN ARAMAIC PALIMPSEST

This text by Saint John Chrysostom 'Homily on the Prodigal Son' (New Finds Sp. 7) is written in descendant of the language which Jesus will have used.

A second text has been written over the original: this recycling of earlier materials is surprisingly common.

century remains a mystery to this day, but the secret may well still have been known to Sergius of Resh'aina (died 536), who made the earlier of two Syriac translations of the work, uniquely preserved in a manuscript (Syriac ms 52) in the monastery's collection. Of particular significance among the New Finds is a rare illustration in a biblical manuscript dating from before the iconoclast period: a full-standing portrait of King David, clad in royal purple, holding his harp in one hand and a book (presumably the Psalms) in the other.

For the study of early Christian and Arabic literature the monastery's extensive collection of Arabic manuscripts is of outstanding importance. Subsequent to the advent of Islam, the use of Arabic as a literary language by both Christians and Muslims seems to have been pioneered by monks of the monasteries of the Judaean Desert, such as those of Saint Sabbas and Saint Chariton, in the eighth and ninth centuries. Some of the earliest products of this innovative literary movement are preserved in manuscripts dating from the ninth and tenth centuries — remarkably early for Arabic manuscripts of any sort; among the New Finds is one dated as early as 859. Though the majority of these texts are translations from Greek or Syriac, some were originally composed in Arabic.

Although considerably smaller in size, the Georgian collection is likewise of great significance, for it is unique in preserving Georgian manuscripts of the ninth and tenth centuries containing translations from Greek by Georgian-speaking monks living in Palestinian monasteries. The name of one Georgian scribe, John Zosimos, has already been mentioned: he was active at the end of the tenth century, first at the Monastery of Saint Sabbas and later at Saint Catherine's, and is well known from the colophons he left at the end of manuscripts he copied. One of the most remarkable items in the Georgian collection is a psalter on papyrus of the seventh or eighth century, unfortunately very damaged.

Christian Palestinian Aramaic is one of the few known descendants of the Aramaic of first-century Palestine, the

language which Jesus will have spoken; it came to be written down, in its own distinctive script, in the fifth or sixth century, and continued in use as a literary and liturgical language for the Aramaic-speaking Orthodox population of Palestine until the end of the thirteenth century, when it was replaced entirely by Arabic. Manuscripts in this dialect are extremely rare, and the majority of those that do survive are either in, or once belonged to, the Monastery of Saint Catherine. The texts they contain are all translations from Greek (biblical, liturgical and patristic).

Slav monastic centres are known to have been in existence in the Holy Land and in Sinai by the early thirteenth century, and it is probably from such communities that Saint Catherine's fine collection of Slavonic manuscripts derives. The oldest, from the eleventh and twelfth centuries, are in the ancient Glagolitic script invented by Saint Cyril and Saint Methodius; a curiosity among the New Finds of Slavonic

95

manuscripts in this script is a psalter with a collection of practical remedies against poisons added at the end.

Among the languages for which the monastery has much smaller holdings of manuscripts, three fragmentary Latin manuscripts of the ninth or tenth century deserve special mention. One of these, a psalter, is known to have already been in the monastery in the early thirteenth century; it is probable that all the Latin manuscripts originate from the same place, and idiosyncratic features suggest they may come from a Latin-speaking monastery in North Africa.

Quite a number of manuscripts contain a note at the end threatening those who remove them without permission with excommunication or dire curses. Unfortunately this has in many cases proved an insufficient precaution against human predators, and it is evident that already in the eighteenth century the monastery's library was at risk from acquisitive European visitors. The worst period, however, was from the mid-nineteenth century until the early years of the present century. Von Tischendorf's underhand 'borrowing' of the Codex Sinaiticus has already been mentioned; on an earlier visit in 1844 he had persuaded the monastery to part with a few folios of the same manuscript; these are now to be found in Leipzig, along with a number of other early biblical fragments he obtained from Saint Catherine's. Even before von Tischendorf's first visit, Porfirij Uspenskij had persuaded the monastery to let him return home to Russia with a haul of mementos from his visit, among them a fine psalter of 862 now known as the Uspensky Psalter, thirteen leaves of which are still preserved in the monastery, having come to light among the New Finds.

Other manuscripts, or fragments of manuscripts (sometimes flagrantly cut out), were surreptitiously stolen by visitors to the library, eventually ending up in western European and American collections: thus there are today fragments definitely originating from Saint Catherine's to be found in libraries in Birmingham, Bryn Mawr, Cambridge, Cincinnati, Göttingen, Graz, Leiden, Leipzig, London, Milan, Saint Petersburg, Rome, Strasbourg, Tbilisi and elsewhere. Lamentably, some which were eventually bought by Louvain University were destroyed in a bombing raid during the Second World War.

But to end on a happier note, it is worth recording that, just occasionally, stolen material was actually returned to the monastery: thanks to the vigilance of the Scottish twin sisters Mrs Agnes Lewis and Mrs Margaret Gibson (who catalogued the monastery's Syriac and Arabic manuscripts in 1894), a Cairo dealer was caught red-handed with a Syriac manuscript that Mrs Lewis recognized as belonging to the monastery; nevertheless, even after a court case, the monastery was only able to recover the manuscript (in 1901) by buying it back from the court for quite a large sum. It was also thanks to a note published by Mrs Lewis in an academic journal that a leaf from the Syriac Sinaiticus Gospels, which she had discovered to have gone missing since her previous visit, was eventually returned, for it is now to be found in its proper place in the manuscript.

98

An Unrivalled Record of the Icon Painter's Art

GEORGE GALAVRIS

FROM EARLY CHRISTIAN TIMES, ICONS WERE VITAL to the life of the Monastery of Saint Catherine: essential to the celebration of the divine liturgy, they were also an important adjunct to the prayers of the faithful. The sheer number of religious images to be seen at the monastery filled the early pilgrims with awe. Of particular renown were the 'itineraries', or miracle-working icons, which were displayed on the *proskynetarion* (icon stand) or on the walls of the basilica, and in the numerous chapels that marked the way to the summit of Mount Sinai.

In the early days of the monastery, some of the icons must have come from monastic houses in the imperial capital of Constantinople. Soon, however, the monks of Saint Catherine's began producing their own holy images. Thus, in the course of more than 1,400 years, an unparalleled icon collection was built up and preserved. Saint Catherine's collection of more than two thousand icons is unique, representing as it does an unbroken record of Orthodox painting from the sixth to the twentieth centuries.

The first academic to draw proper attention to the Sinai icons was Professor Constantinos Amantos. He was followed by two great Greek scholars, George and Maria Sotiriou. In 1938 they were invited by the monastery to study the icons, and the publication of their research in a two-volume reference work was a landmark in the history of Saint Catherine's icon collection. It was this that prompted the American Kurt Weitzmann to organize a series of expeditions to Saint Catherine's from the universities of Michigan, Princeton and Alexandria, with the participation of Greek scholars of the stature of Manolis Chatzidakis.

CHRIST PANTOCRATOR *(Christ as Ruler of the Universe)*
This encaustic icon of Christ is one of the earliest at the Monastery of Saint Catherine. It was painted in the first half of the sixth century in Constantinople by an artist who has succeeded in rendering both Christ's divinity and his humanity in one impressive image. It may well reflect the famous icon of Christ placed over the Chalke Gate in Constantinople.

99

SAINT PETER

One of the earliest representations of Saint Peter is shown in this Constantinopolitan encaustic icon of the late sixth or early seventh century. Above the saint are three medallions with Christ in the centre, Mary to the right and Saint John the Evangelist to the left. Such compositions were based on the familiar iconography of consular diptychs.

A highlight of the collection is the group of early Christian panels painted before the restoration of the icons in AD 843, that is prior to the triumph of orthodoxy over iconoclasm. The isolation of the monastery ensured

KING ABGARUS
Many of Sinai's icons show stories from the Lives of the Saints. In this example that is made from two separate wings of a triptych we see King Abgarus of Edessa (top right) holding the cloth with the miraculous imprint of the face of Christ (the Mandelion) brought to him from Jerusalem by Ananias. These wings were painted in the middle of the tenth century.

the continued survival and production of icons in the Sinai at a time when eastern Christianity deemed images of Christ, the Virgin Mary, and the saints to be idolatrous. Following the Arab conquest of the Sinai in AD 641, and throughout the iconoclastic period (726-842), Saint Catherine's remained outside the orbit of Byzantium, a lone bastion of the Orthodox faith in an Islamic world. As such, the monastery was not subject to the decrees of the Byzantine emperors.

The earliest of Saint Catherine's icons are in the encaustic technique: coloured wax, melted on heated metal palettes, was laid by brush on a wooden panel and retouched with heated irons. Outstanding among these panels is the icon

THE NATIVITY
A detail from an iconostasis beam which once formed the left and central portion of the original three part beam.

of *Christ Pantocrator* (Christ as Ruler of the Universe) of the first half of the sixth century. The figure of Christ is set against a niche, which creates the impression of space. While the majestic pose symbolizes Christ's divine nature, the naturalistic rendering of the face suggests His humanity.

According to tradition, Christ's features evoke miraculously formed images such as that of the cloth of Kamouliani in Cappadocia. The panel at Saint Catherine's may well recall the famous icon of Christ (destroyed in 726) set above the doors of the Chalke Gate at Constantinople, as Manolis Chatzidakis has proposed. The icon of *Christ Pantocrator* was probably given to the monastery by the emperor, together with another fine panel portraying *Saint*

Peter as an intellectual and prince of the Church. One of the earliest representations of that saint, the icon dates from the late sixth or early seventh century.

Icons produced at Saint Catherine's during the iconoclastic period show affinities with the art of Palestine and Coptic Egypt. An example of the latter, *The three Hebrews in the fiery furnace* (seventh century, assigned to Palestine), displays motifs typical of Coptic frescoes from Saqqara and Nubia, such as the angel holding a long staff terminating in a cross. An eighth-century icon of the *Crucifixion* made in Palestine for the monastery is the earliest known portrayal of Christ on the cross, wearing a crown of thorns.

From the second half of the ninth century onwards, the

THE TRANSFIGURATION
The right hand section would have shown more scenes from the Twelve Great Feasts of Orthodoxy (the Dodekaorton). This large work of the late twelfth century was probably intended for the main templon of the basilica.

influx of Constantinopolitan art and its influence on iconography and style are again evident at Saint Catherine's. The tenth-century icon with Abgarus is characteristically Constantinopolitan in its brilliant, enamel-like colours and the classical poses of the figures. This, the oldest representation of the story of Abgarus, king of Edessa, has been related to the Byzantine cult of relics and the Emperor Constantine Porphyrogenitos, whose portrait is seen in the face of Abgarus, as Kurt Weitzmann has shown.

A group of eleventh-and twelfth-century icons produced at or for Saint Catherine's relate to illustrated manuscripts

in the monastery's collection. The numerous *icons-menologia*, or calendar icons — of which Saint Catherine's has the oldest and richest collection — depict the saints whose festivals take place within a given calendar month. These icons are astonishing for the minuteness of the work and the mastery of their execution.

Some of the early *iconostasis epistylia* (painted icon-screen panels) with images of the *Deesis* (Christ with the Virgin and John the Baptist) and *Dodekaorton* (the twelve main Church feasts celebrating twelve important events in the life of Christ figure among the great masterpieces of Constan-

THE VIRGIN OF THE
BURNING BUSH
*flanked by four monastic
Saints of Sinai. This
thirteenth century work is the
only icon which in its
inscription records the name
of the iconographic type
known as the Virgin of the
Burning Bush which enjoyed
special honour at Saint
Catherine's.*

tinopolitan art. These images also provide the basis for the study of the development of the icon-screen in the Greek Church. A late twelfth-century *Annunciation* from the Dodekaorton typifies the Constantinopolitan style: the Virgin Mary has a warm, human expression, whereas the angel recalls the ecstatic dancers of ancient art. Of the three painters responsible for the so-called *Epistylion of the three masters* (circa 1300), the most innovative in mode of expression is a great artist. He animates figures and landscapes with a vibrant, impressionistic brushstroke, giving eloquent form to a deeply felt religious experience.

Certain icons attest to the artistic links that existed between Saint Catherine's and Cyprus, where the monastery had property. The larger icons of Cypriot provenance were most likely substitutes for wall paintings in the Catholikon, the basilica of the monastery, and its many chapels.

A special Sinaitic iconography developed at Saint Catherine's in the twelfth century, when the monks first depicted the holy sites that surrounded them and the ascetics and martyrs of the monastery. These icons constitute an important record of the history of Saint Catherine's and the cult of its saints. A recurrent theme is the Virgin of the Burning Bush accompanied by the saints of the Sinai. Saint Catherine's image began to appear on icons with the transfer of her relics to the monastery, some time after the tenth century. *Saint Catherine and Saint Marina,* the earliest representation of the monastery's patroness, dates from the late tenth or early eleventh century.

In the early part of the thirteenth century, the Monastery of Saint Catherine continued to produce icons of high quality; however, from about the middle of the century, with the appearance of what Weitzmann has termed the 'Crusader' style, a period of stagnation set in. Crusader icons combine Byzantine and western elements. They may have Latin inscriptions, for example, like the double-sided icon of the *Crucifixion* and *Resurrection,* probably the product of a Venetian workshop. According to one view, these icons may have been made by Italian and French artists, who followed the Crusaders to the Holy Land and took up residence in the monastery, where they were influenced by the Byzantine style. Alternatively, these icons may have been painted by Greeks who tried to imitate western works.

While contact with the West continued during the fourteenth and fifteenth centuries, icons produced then depended once again on the art of Constantinople. Evidently the fall of the imperial capital in 1454 had no effect on the production of religious images at Sinai or its various *metochia*. Increasingly, however, the influence of the Cretan school became apparent, as in a *Lamentation* of the early fifteenth century. The *Deesis* by a great Cretan painter known as Angelos, who worked in the second quarter of

SAINT CATHERINE AND
SAINT MARINA
This icon carries a very early representation of Saint Catherine, the monastery's patroness.

the fifteenth century, is a splendid example of his art, notable for the beauty and nobility of the faces and the lyricism of the handling.

At the end of the sixteenth century Cretan icon painters impressed by the Italian mannerist style introduced mannerism into their work, bringing together East and West, the transcendental world of Byzantium and the naturalistic European world. A good representative of this trend is Georgios Klontzos, who painted the icon entitled *Monastic Life*.

Post-Byzantine Cretan icons with special significance for Saint Catherine's include works of the seventeenth century

DEESIS
This beautiful Deesis from the middle of the fifteenth is the work of the Cretan painter Angelos, to whom more than forty signed and unsigned works are attributed.
Here we can see his signature to the bottom right of the panel. This finely worked icon radiates a noble and gentle dignity.

Facing page:
THE ANASTASIS
(the Resurrection) the reverse of a two-sided icon of Venetian origin, shows many western features including the pink mandorla of Christ, the punched haloes, the golden stars against the deep blue background and the strongly realistic rendering of the figures.

attributed to Victor, a Cretan priest. Notable for their Sinaitic iconography, these icons portray events relating to the Sinai's holy sites. The earliest and best known depiction of the Sinai landscape is the famous diptych at Modena by El Greco, which served as a model for icons produced at Saint Catherine's by Cretan artists. Adopted by painters in the monastery, the theme was disseminated to Russia and Georgia. However, this opens another chapter in the history of Saint Catherine's, one featuring the monastery's relations with the Russian tsars and the Gospodars of Wallachia.

From the days of its foundation, the Monastery of Saint Catherine stood at the crossroads of history, faith and taste. The icons in the monastery collection reflect the extraordinary cultural diversity that characterizes the long history of Saint Catherine's.

A Brief Chronology relating to the Monastery of Saint Catherine's

306-312 AD	*Martyrdom of Saint Catherine of Alexandria*
380	*Christianity becomes the religion of the Roman Empire*
384	*Etheria makes her pilgrimage to Mount Sinai*
527	*Emperor Justinian builds the fortified monastery at the foot of Mount Sinai*
550-600	*Mosaic of the Transfiguration made in the church*
570	*Birth of Mohammed in Mecca*
638	*Muslims capture Jerusalem*
726-842	*The Iconoclast Controversy*
968	*Vladimir of Kiev introduces the Orthodox Religion into his lands*
1025	*Relics of Saint Catherine brought to Rouen Cathedral: the spread of the cult of Saint Catherine*
1054	*The Eastern Orthodox Church becomes completely independent*
1096-1291	*The Crusades*
1453	*The Turks take Constantinople*
1483	*Friar Felix Fabri visits Sinai*
1517	*Sinai taken by the Turks*
1738	*Bishop Pococke visits Saint Catherine's Monastery*
1798	*Egypt taken by the French* *Napoleon places Saint Catherine's under his protection, damaged walls rebuilt in 1801*
1816	*John Lewis Burckhardt visits Saint Catherine's*
1839	*David Roberts makes drawings of the monastery*
1859	*The Codex Sinaiticus is taken from the monastery*
1871	*Bell Tower built containing 9 bells presented by the tsars of Russia*
1917	*The annual Imperial Russian supply caravan from Cairo terminated*
1934	*Chapel rebuilt on the summit of Mount Sinai*

Further reading

Burckhardt, John Lewis, *Travels in Syria and the Holy Land,* London, John Murray, 1822

Dobson, A. M. R., *Mount Sinai: a modern pilgrimage,* London, 1925

Galey, John, *Sinai and the Monastery of Saint Catherine,* Cairo, American University in Cairo Press, 1985

Hobbs, Joseph J., *Mount Sinai,* Austin, University of Texas Press, 1995. *Contains an extensive bibliography*

Laborde, Leon de, *Journey through Arabia Pertæa to Mount Sinai…,* London, John Murray, 1836

Manafis, Konstantinos A., ed. *Sinai: Treasures of the Monastery of Saint Catherine,* Athens, Ekdotike Athenon, 1990

Pococke, Richard, *Description of the East and some other countries,* London, W. Bowyer, 1743

Prescott, H. F. M., *Once to Sinai: The further pilgrimage of Friar Felix Fabbri,* London, Eyre and Spottiswoode, 1957

Roberts, David, *The Holy Land,* London, F. G. Moon, 1842-49

Contributors

DR SEBASTIAN BROCK
is Reader in Syriac Studies at the Oriental Institute, University of Oxford. His most recent publication is the Catalogue of Syriac Fragments which form part of the 'New Finds' of the Library of the Monastery of Saint Catherine.

PROFESSOR GEORGE GALAVARIS
is Professor of Art History at McGill University, Canada. He has studied the icons at Saint Catherine's over many years, and his many publications reflect this interest.

EVE GRAVES
is Senior Lecturer in the History of Art and Design at the London Institute, Camberwell College of Arts. She has worked for over twenty years in the field of medieval studies with a particular interest in popular culture and pilgrimage.

RICHARD HUGHES
is Dean of Art History and Conservation at the London Institute, Camberwell College of Arts. In 1995 he led a team from Camberwell College of Arts that conducted a conservation survey at Saint Catherine's Monastery.

PROFESSOR CYRIL MANGO
is Bywater and Sotheby Professor Emeritus of Byzantine and Modern Greek Languages and Literature, University of Oxford.

PROFESSOR ORIANA BADDELEY
is Course Director of History of Art and Design at the London Institute, Camberwell College of Arts, and co-curator of the Saint Catherine's Exhibition to be held at the Foundation for Hellenic Culture, London.

EARLEEN BRUNNER
has worked as an editor for *The Burlington Magazine* and Berlitz Publications. She is now a freelance editor based in Geneva.

Index

Entries in italic refer to illustration captions